freytag & berndt

— TRAVEL GUIDE —
PRAGUE

Sixty-four of the loveliest spots in the Czech metropolis

PRAGUE
Travel Guide

2nd edition, 2016
Published by freytag & berndt Praha
Sodomkova 1558/12, 102 00 Praha 10
tel.: 226 200 358, fax: 226 200 359
e-mail: obchod@freytagberndt.cz
www.freytagberndt.cz

Photo on cover: © Jaroslav Kocourek
Editing, graphic design, layout, cover: freytag & berndt Praha
Print: PBtisk Příbram

© freytag & berndt
Mechanical, photographic or electronic reproduction of the work or part thereof only with expressed written consent of the authors.

ISBN 978-80-7445-120-1

Basic Introduction

Vltava river.

Prague is one of the Czech Republic's most attractive cities, welcoming millions of tourists each year from around the world to admire its monuments. Prague's singularity as an architectural and cultural jewel is seen through its many nicknames – "the city of 100 spires" for its countless towers and spires shooting above city rooftops, "golden" for its Rudolfian-era riches, the "heart of Europe" for its central position on the continent, the "Rome of the north" for the nine hills around which it's built, and the "pearl of cities" for its unmatched beauty. Many important personalities have expressed this in the past, like German poet Johann Wolfgang Goethe, who declared that "in the crown of cities, this is the most precious stone". Prague truly holds an interesting position amongst other European and world metropolises. It is extraordinary for its picturesque setting amongst hills rising on both sides of the Vltava, whose course holds several islands, and for its terrain diversity forming many dramatic panoramas. Nearly every visitor has strolled along Smetana Embankment at least once to enjoy the iconic view of Charles Bridge and the line of palaces of Prague Castle rising above it with the towers of St. Vitus Cathedral. Amazing views of Prague also await visitors from several monuments built atop these hills – like from Prague Castle, the Petřín Lookout Tower or from Vyšehrad. Thanks to its long history, Prague boasts a unique group of monuments. Its historical center was listed as a UNESCO World Cultural and Natural Heritage Site in 1992.

Contents

Basic Introduction	3
Useful Information	10
Prague Castle	**21**
1 St. Vitus Cathedral	22
2 St. George's Basilica	23
3 Castle Palaces and Courtyards	24
4 Royal Summer Palace	25
5 Golden Lane	26
Bridges	**27**
6 Charles Bridge	28
7 Čech Bridge	29
8 Hlávka Bridge	30
Quarters and Squares	**31**
9 Old Town Square	32
10 Josefov	33
11 Old Jewish Cemetery	34
12 Wenceslas Square	35
13 Charles Square	36
14 Vyšehrad Cemetery and Slavín	37
15 Olšany Cemetery	38
Chateaux and Summer Palaces	**39**
16 Troja Chateau	40
17 Governor's Summer Palace in Stromovka	41
18 Hvězda Summer Residence	42
19 Kinský Summer Palace	43
20 Bertramka	44
Palaces	**45**
21 Archbishop's Palace	46
22 Wallenstein Palace	47
23 Černín Palace	48
24 Schwarzenberg Palace	49
25 Lobkowicz Palace	50
Monasteries	**51**
26 St. Agnes of Bohemia Convent	52
27 Strahov Monastery	53
28 Břevnov Monastery	54
Churches	**55**
29 Church of Our Lady before Týn	56

30	St. Nicholas Church (Lesser Side)	57
31	Church of Our Lady of Victory (Carmelite)	58
32	Church of St. Wenceslas of Smíchov	59
33	Church of the Sacred Heart	60

Modern Architecture — 61

34	Villa Bílek	62
35	Koruna Palace	63
36	House of the Black Madonna	64
37	Villa Müller	65
38	The Dancing House	66

Technical Monuments — 67

39	Astronomical Clock	68
40	Loreto – Chimes	69
41	Petřín Observation Tower and Funicular	70
42	Žižkov Tower	71
43	Podolí Water Treatment Plant	72
44	Prague Main Train Station	73
45	Sewage Treatment Plant in Bubeneč	74

Museums and Galleries — 75

46	National Museum	76
47	City of Prague Museum	77
48	Vítkov National Monument	78
49	Museum of Decorative Arts	79
50	National Gallery – Trade Fair Palace	80
51	Kampa Museum	81
52	Museum of Public Transportation in Prague	82

Cultural Institutions — 83

53	National Theater	84
54	Theater of the Estates	85
55	State Opera	86
56	Rudolfinum	87
57	Klementinum	88
58	Municipal House	89
59	Hybernia Theater	90

Natural Monuments — 91

60	Zoo	92
61	Prague Botanical Garden	93
62	Wallenstein Garden	94
63	Stromovka	95
64	Gardens under Prague Castle	96

Useful Information

Hradčany in autumn.

Prague City Tourism – tourist information service

www.prague.eu, e-mail: tourinfo@prague.eu

These centers provide all tourist information about Prague – monuments, cultural program, social events, transportation, accommodations, entertainment centers, shopping network, sports and orientation in the city.
Sale: city tours and trips, boat rides, Segway tours, bicycle tours, tickets to cultural events, guides and information brochures about Prague, city maps, CDs, DVDs, post cards, city transport timed tickets, telephone cards, Prague Card – 2/4-day entrance ticket to 50 places in Prague.

- **Old Town Hall,** Prague 1, Staroměstské náměstí 1, Mon–Sun 9:00 a.m. – 7:00 p.m.
- **Prague 1, Rytířská 12**, Mon–Sun 10:00 a.m. – 6:00 p.m.
- **Small Town Bridge Tower**, Prague 1, Charles Bridge, Mon–Sun 10:00 a.m. – 6:00 p.m. (IV–X)
- **Václav Havel Airport Prague**, arrivals hall Terminal 2, Prague 6-Ruzyně, Mon–Sun 8:00 a.m. – 8:00 p.m.

Charles Bridge.

CzechTourism – information center

www.czechtourism.com

Promotional and information material about Prague and the Czech Republic, information on accommodations, transport and cultural events.
- Prague 2, Vinohradská 46, tel.: 221 580 611,
  e-mail: info@czechtourism.cz, Mon–Fri 8:30 a.m. – 12:00 p.m., 1:00 p.m. – 4:00 p.m.
- Prague 1, Staroměstské nám. 5, tel.: 224 861 476, www.czechtourism.com,
  e-mail: staromestska@czechtourism.cz, in season Mon–Fri 9.00 a.m. – 5.00 p.m.,
  Sat–Sun 10:00 a.m. – 5:00 p.m., out of season Mon–Fri 9:00 a.m. – 5:00 p.m.,
  Sat–Sun 10:00 a.m. – 3:00 p.m.

PRAGUE CARD – Prague tourist card

www.praguecitycard.com

2/4-day card providing tourists access to roughly 50 sites, including a series of important Prague museums and monuments. It also includes a free two-hour tour of the historic city centre, public transport and transfer to the airport.
There are several versions of the Prague Card on offer: two days for CZK 1,280, three days for CZK 1,540 or four days for CZK 1,780 Discounts are provided to children and students.
The card can be purchased at all information centers of the Prague Information Service (Old Town Hall, Lesser Town Bridge Tower, Rytířská 12, Václav Havel Airport Prague), also e.g. in branches of the Čedok travel agency (Nekázanka 2, Rytířská 16, Loretánské nám. 3) or in the information center at the Prague-Florenc bus station.

MONUMENT TOURS

Dispatching for foreign language guides
Prague City Tourism – Pragotur
Qualified guides in many European languages for basic and specialized tours around Prague, walking tours and excursions out to the surroundings. Option of preparing a program as you wish, even with transportation.
Prague 1, Staroměstské náměstí 1 (Old Town Hall), tel.: 236 002 562, 236 002 569,
e-mail: guides@prague.eu

Bicycle tours of Prague
Prague Bike
www.prahabike.cz

Rides through the city, out to the surroundings, bicycle rental.
Prague 1, Dlouhá 24, tel.: 732 388 880, Mon–Sun 9:00 a.m. – 8:00 p.m.

Boat excursions along the Vltava
Pražská paroplavební společnost
www.paroplavba.cz

Excursions to Mělník and to Slapy Reservoir, boat sight-seeing tours of central Prague, trip to the zoo. Possible to combine with on-board lunch or dinner.
Prague 2, Rašínovo nábřeží, steamship port between Palacký and Jirásek Bridge,
tel.: 224 931 013, 224 930 017, e-mail: pps@paroplavba.cz

Old-New Synagogue.

EVD
Sightseeing cruises, local tours and rental of restaurant boats.
Prague 1, Dvořákovo nábřeží (by Čech Bridge), tel.: 224 810 030, 605 700 007, www.evd.cz,
e-mail: evd@paroplavba.cz

SERVICE

IMPORTANT TELEPHONE NUMBERS
Emergency calls	112
Fire	150
Police	158
Paramedics	155
Medical emergency (Palackého 5)	224 949 181
Dental emergency (Palackého 5)	224 949 181
Non-stop pharmacy (Palackého 5)	224 946 982
Accident service (automobiles)	ÚAMK 1230, ABA 1240
Telephone directory assistance	1180

HOLIDAYS

January 1 – Restoration Day of the Independent Czech State, New Year
Easter Monday
May 1 – May Day
May 8 – Liberation Day
July 5 – Saints Cyril and Methodius Day
July 6 – Jan Hus Day
September 28 – Czech Statehood Day
October 28 – Independent Czechoslovak State Day
November 17 – Struggle for Freedom and Democracy Day
December 24 – Christmas Eve
December 25 – Christmas Day
December 26 – St. Stephen's Day

Offices and banks are closed on Saturdays, Sundays and state holidays. Ordinary shops are also closed on Sundays and state holidays, while supermarkets and hypermarkets generally stay open without limitation. State and other holidays are not working days.

BANKS AND CURRENCY EXCHANGE OFFICES

Like other large European cities, Prague has a significant number of banks, mainly in the city center it is no problem to handle your financial matters. It generally applies that banks are open from Monday to Thursday 8:30 a.m. to 5:00 p.m., closing earlier on Friday. Most banks also operate an exchange office, with only slight differences in the daily official exchange

The Municipal House.

rate. Classic exchange offices can be found mainly in the city center at tourist-frequented places. They are open each day from roughly 8:00 a.m. to 10:00 p.m., but some are nonstop. Most hotels also offer currency exchange services.

CZECH POST OFFICE

www.ceskaposta.cz

Certain post office branches in the center are open from Monday to Friday from 8:00 a.m. to 7:00 p.m. or 8:00 p.m., e.g. Kaprova 12, tel.: 224 811 261 or Hybernská 15, tel.: 224 219 714. The main post office in the city center is open each day almost non-stop (Mon–Sun 2:00 a.m. –12:00 a.m.): Prague 1, Jindřišská 14, tel.: 221 131 111.
Also open every day is the post office at Prague Castle, Courtyard III, tel. 257 320 778 (Mon–Fri 8:00 a.m. – 6:00 p.m., Sat–Sun 10:00 a.m. – 6:00 p.m.).

TRANSPORT

www.dpp.cz

City public transport (CPT)
Prague Public Transit Company
Information: tel.: 296 19 18 17 (Mon–Sun 7:00 a.m. – 9:00 p.m.)
Traffic Information Center (TIC):
metro station A/C: Muzeum, Mon–Sun 7:00 a.m. – 9:00 p.m.
metro station A: Hradčanská, Mon–Fri 6:00 a.m. – 8:00 p.m., Sat–Sun 9:30 a.m. – 5:00 p.m.
metro station A: Nádraží Veleslavín, Mon–Fri 6:00 a.m. – 8:00 p.m., Sat 9:30 a.m. – 5:00 p.m.
metro station B: Můstek (Prague City Hall), Mon–Thu 8:00 a.m. – 6:00 p.m.,
Fri 8:00 a.m. – 4:00 p.m.
metro station B: Anděl, Mon–Fri 7:00 a.m. – 9:00 p.m., Sat–Sun 9:30 a.m. – 5:00 p.m.

Underground station Depo Hostivař. *Tram Škoda 14 T in Prague.*

metro station C: Hlavní nádraží (Main Train Station), Mon–Sun 7:00 a.m. – 9:00 p.m.
Václav Havel Airport Prague – terminal 1, Mon–Sun 7:00 a.m. – 9:00 p.m.
Václav Havel Airport Prague – terminal 2, Mon–Sun 7:00 a.m. – 9:00 p.m.

Metro
The Prague city metro network is comprised of three lines marked by letters and colors: **A-Green Line** (Nemocnice Motol – Depo Hostivař), **B-Yellow Line** (Černý Most – Zličín), **C-Red Line** (Letňany – Háje). Transfers between lines are possible in the stations Muzeum (A/C), Můstek (A/B) and Florenc (B/C). The metro runs every day from 5:00 a.m. to 12:00 a.m. The time interval between trains during rush hour is 2–3 minutes, otherwise 4–10 minutes.

Trams
Most tram lines run through the city center. Daily lines no. 1–36 operate from 4:30 a.m. to 12:15 a.m. Intervals on individual lines are mostly between 8 and 15 minutes, with half that interval on the most frequent, so-called backbone lines (no. 9, 17 and 22). Night operation is provided by lines no. 51–59 in 30-minute intervals. The central transfer stop for night lines is Lazarská. The historical line no. 91 operates **from April until mid-November** on Saturdays, Sundays and holidays **from 12:00 p.m.** until around **5:35 p.m.**
Tram timetables are found at all stops. Be careful...trams ALWAYS have the right of way even at pedestrian crossings!

Buses
Buses provide transport services mainly in the city periphery. Daily (**4:30 a.m. – 12:15 a.m.**, Fri-Sat from **4:30 a.m. to 1:30 a.m.**) and night operation is similar to that of the trams; at night the lines no. 501–515 run with an interval of 30/60 minutes. Bus timetables are also found at all stops.

Petřín Funicular
At the top of Petřín Hill, you can take the scenic funicular along the route Újezd – Nebozízek – Petřín. In operation daily.

Prague bus.

The funicular on Petřín hill.

April–October 9:00 a.m. – 11:30 p.m., interval 10 min., November–March 9:00 a.m. – 11:20 p.m., interval 15 min.,
the ride takes 4 minutes, to the stop Nebozízek just 2 minutes. Two cars go up 130 m, and the track length is 510 m. Undergoing reconstruction work from 7. 9. 2015 to 18. 3. 2016 and therefore not in service.

Ferries
An interesting means of transport that is incorporated into the city transport system is ferry transport connecting both banks of the Vltava.

P1 Sedlec – Zámky: year-long operation
P2 V Podbabě – Podhoří: year-long operation
P3 Lihovar – Veslařský ostrov: seasonal operation April–October
P5 Kotevní – Císařská louka – Výtoň: seasonal operation April–October
P6 Lahovičky – Nádraží Modřany: operation April–mid-December
Fare is the same as with other means of Prague public transport. Bicycle transport incurs no extra charge.

Fares in City Public Transport
Traveling by city public transport is only possible with a valid ticket purchased by passengers prior to entering the vehicle or transport areas of the metro. The ticket is only valid if it has been validated by stamping in the provided machines. Tickets are sold in selected metro stations, in newspaper and magazine stands, in the transport company information centers, in hotels, at travel agencies, etc. Tickets for a single ride can also be obtained in automatic machines located in all metro stations, near certain stations of surface transport or for a higher rate, directly with the driver (only applies to bus transport).

SMS ticket
You can also buy a ticket by means of an SMS message, which you send as "DPT + the price of the selected ticket" (DPT32, DPT24, DPT110, DPT310) to the number 902 06. Within

around two minutes, you will receive your ticket by SMS. Travelers using this service must enter the vehicle or transport areas of the metro only with the SMS ticket already received on their mobile phones!

Types of fares
Basic fare – CZK 32 (discounted for children aged 6–15 and seniors aged 60–70: CZK 16) – The ticket is valid for 90 minutes from validation for all types of CPT.

Short-term fare – CZK 24 (discounted for children aged 6–15 and seniors aged 60–70: CZK 12) – The ticket is valid for 30 minutes from validation for all types of CPT.

Tourist tickets
24 hours (1 day) – CZK 110
72 hours (3 days) – CZK 310

Free transport
Those traveling free are e.g. children up to 6 years of age, baby carriages, animals in a pet travel container, and bicycles (only in the metro).

Control of tickets
Controllers of the Prague Public Transit Company may check the validity of tickets at any time during the ride or while passengers are within the transport areas of the metro. In case a passenger is found not to have a valid ticket, the controller is authorized to issue a fine in the amount of CZK 1,000 (CZK 800 if paying on the spot). The controller will prove his/her identity by displaying a yellow-red badge and service ID card.

TAXI

Prague offers a sufficient amount of taxis both day and night. Prior to traveling, it is necessary to know certain principles that will help you avoid unpleasant situations or surprises. Prague has taxi service operators whose fleet differs in quality and color. One thing applies to all of them – that they must be visibly marked by the word TAXI on the vehicle roof along with the name, registration number and prices on the doors. Inside the vehicle, there must be the driver's ID card and the taxi meter must be running, from which you will receive a receipt upon arriving at your destination.

Maximum prices for Prague taxi services:
ride within Prague city limits CZK 28/1 km
boarding fee CZK 40
waiting CZK 6/1 min
If the driver charges more or refuses to issue a receipt, you have probably just been victimized by a swindler. Do not pay the fine and call Prague Municipal Police at the number 156.

RAILWAY TRANSPORT

www.cd.cz

Czech Railways (České dráhy), information on train connections nonstop –
tel.: 840 112 113

Important train stations
Main Train Station, Prague 2, Wilsonova street, metro C: Prague Main Train Station
Masaryk Train Station, Prague 1, Hybernská street, metro B: Republic Square
Smíchov Train Station, Prague 5, Nádražní street, metro B: Smíchov Train Station
Holešovice Train Station, Prague 7, Partyzánská street, metro C: Holešovice Train Station

BUS TRANSPORT

www.jizdnirady.cz

Information on bus connections nonstop – tel.: 900 144 444
Important bus stations
Florenc, Prague 8, Křižíkova street, metro B/C: Florenc, www.florenc.cz
Na Knížecí, Prague 5, Nádražní street, metro B: Anděl
Holešovice, Prague 7, Partyzánská street, metro C: Holešovice Train Station
Roztyly, Prague 4, Ryšavého street, metro C: Roztyly
Černý Most, Prague 9, Chlumecká street, metro B: Černý Most

Fast train Super City Pendolino.

Václav Havel Airport Prague.

AIR TRANSPORT

www.csl.cz

Václav Havel Airport Prague – Ruzyně
Information on departures and arrivals at tel.: 220 113 314
Czech Airlines (ČSA)
Information, reservations and ticket sales (in person) – Prague 1, V Celnici 5, Mon–Fri 9:30 a.m. – 5:00 p.m.
Contact center – tel.: 239 007 007, www.csa.cz

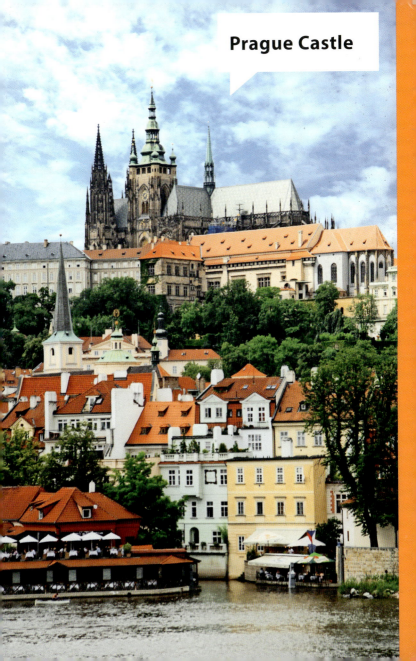

Prague Castle

1. St. Vitus Cathedral
⌖ 50°5′27.16″N, 14°24′2.14″E

The panorama of Hradčany would be far less stunning without St. Vitus, St. Wenceslas and St. Adalbert Cathedral, the name of the nation's loveliest and most important church since 1997. The grand Gothic structure stands at the spot of the former St. Vitus Rotunda. It was built by Prince Wenceslas around 927 and it is also his final resting place. Prince Spytihněv commissioned the larger Romanesque Basilica of St. Vitus, St. Wenceslas and St. Adalbert in 1060. Charles IV and his father Jan of Luxembourg built the existing church in 1344 marking the Prague bishopric's elevation to an archbishopric. The emperor aimed to build not just a worthy Archbishop's church but also a tomb of Czech rulers and place to safely keep rare treasures. But what he certainly didn't intend was for construction to last nearly 600 years. Matyáš of Arras was its first builder. Thus St. Vitus is reminiscent of French Gothic structures. Petr Parléř and his smelting works then took over. Building ceased in the 15th century for several hundred years; serious intentions to complete it only came in the latter-19th century. Architect Josef Mocker drew up plans for finishing the cathedral, and Kamil Hilbert completed it in 1929. It was re-consecrated that year to celebrate the so-called St. Wenceslas millennium. The typical "Parléř interior" had net vaults and a completely new, so-called triforium, a 14.3-meter high walkway above arcades with busts of Charles IV and family members, Prague archbishops, main builders and two of the first architects in the old part, and busts of people involved in new-age completion in its new part. The Chapel of St. Wenceslas is the rarest and holiest of its nearly two-dozen side chapels, with inlaid gems right where St. Wenceslas was laid to rest, and the entrance to the coronation chamber holding the Czech coronation jewels. Seven key personalities (including the president, Prague archbishop, prime minister and others) must meet so that the seven keys could open this chamber. And as the nation's father intended, it also holds the royal tomb, accessible from the Holy Cross Chapel, where he, his four wives and many Czech kings and their relatives rest.

2. St. George's Basilica
50°5'28.26"N, 14°24'9.26"E

PRAGUE CASTLE

For over a millennium an amazing Romanesque monument has stood within Prague Castle complex. St. George Cathedral was founded around 920 by prince Vratislav I, and St. Wenceslas' grandmother was buried here in 925. Later canonized as Princess Ludmila, she and several other princely Přemyslids lie here, as this was the family's official burial site till 1055. Creation of the Prague bishopric in 973 and the first Benedictine nuns' Convent of St. George led to restoring the church into a three-nave, early Romanesque basilica. It looks roughly similar to how it did after a fire in 1142. Two white arenaceous marl towers of varying widths and two rows of Romanesque windows were added. Later centuries saw addition of the Chapel of St. Ludmila (1st half of the 13th century) and the Chapel of St. John of Nepomuk (1st half of the 18th century, architect Ferdinand Maxmilián Kaňka). The 14th-century western façade was restored in early Baroque style in the 17th century, as it looks today. It features a statue of its founder Vratislav I, and founder of the convent, the blessed Mlada, sister of Boleslav II. A copy of an original relief illustrating St. George's fight with a dragon hangs in the tympanum of the south façade on Jiřská street. The austere interior hides valuable remnants of Romanesque frescoes. Walls with arcades and adjoining windows separate the main nave from the side naves. The adjacent St. George Monastery holds some National Gallery collections. Its current exhibit presents 19th-century art collections.

3 Castle Palaces and Courtyards
⊕ 50°5'27.04"N, 14°24'6.36"E

Prague castle is a giant complex of palaces, homes, courtyards and gardens, and it is hard to get to know it all on a short visit. You can enter from many sides. The main entrance, through which official visits arrive, is the 1st Courtyard, surrounded by buildings from the Theresian restoration led by Nicola Pacassi. Going through the originally independently standing Matthias Gate by architect Giovanni Filippi, which Pacassi incorporated into the new buildings, visitors arrive at the 2nd Courtyard with Classicist Holy Cross Chapel, the early Baroque Leopold (also Lion's or Kohl's fountain), a spring and buildings of the New Royal Palace. Another passageway leads you to St. Vitus Cathedral and the observation point of the 3rd Courtyard with the old Probate's office, Plečnik's monolith, fountain and St. George statue. From this courtyard you can go along Bull stairs to the South Gardens or to the Old Royal Palace. The second cellar of the Old Palace hides impressive 12th-century Romanesque areas. The Gothic floor above holds a very interesting permanent exhibit, the Story of Prague Castle. This representative floor's most valuable and largest room is the Vladislav Hall (60 x 16 x 13 m), built at the spot of the former Charles Palace in 1492–1502 based on design by Benedikt Ried (Rejt) in late Gothic style. It has a rich rounded rib vault and the first Renaissance elements north of the Alps – large Italian windows. Visitors enter the Renaissance Ludwig Wing from this hall.

4 Royal Summer Palace
✧ 50°5'37.45"N, 14°24'19.16"E

Ferdinand I. Habsburský (1503–64) decided to expand Prague Castle's complex. To do so, he used the area of the former vineyards above Deer Moat, where he further built a new Royal Garden with rare trees and exotic plant species. Central Europe's first summer palace was built in the eastern part of this garden, used as a residence and for various social events – today's Royal Summer Palace or also Queen Anne's Summer Palace, or Belveder. Experts consider it the loveliest Renaissance architectural achievement, and the purest in style, north of the Alps. Building began in 1538 based on a model and project of Paolo della Stella, a stone mason and sculptor from Italy, who created such works as the reliefs on the walkway arcades. Building was interrupted many times over a lack of money and the castle fire of 1541. This went on until 1563, when the second floor was built. The uniquely shaped copper roof looks somewhat like an overturned ship's keel. Arcades surround the ground floor with living quarters, and a dance hall and gallery are found upstairs. The residence was a Rudolf II-era observatory used by such famous astronomers as Tycho Brahe and Johannes Kepler. The residence's fate thereafter was very unsettled. Swedish forces damaged it and it slowly fell to ruin. The army devastated it under Josef II, and it wasn't restored until the mid-19th century. It was given a monumental staircase and paintings with Czech historical themes on the walls upstairs.

5 Golden Lane
⊕ 50°5'31.17"N, 14°24'14.27"E

The Prague castle complex is not just made up of big palaces and historic churches; it also has a quaint, narrow street with richly painted little houses of various sizes. Benedikt Ried built an outer castle wall around the year 1500. Modest dwellings arose the 16th century in defensive areas behind it belonging to craftsmen, probably mostly goldsmiths as reflected by the lane's name, originally Goldsmith, later Golden. This tiny settlement was apparently razed under Rudolf II upon repairing the walls. But castle guards built new dwellings here upon gaining royal consent. Craftsmen and servants later lived here, eventually followed by the poor. The popular, oftentimes artistically rendered legend that Rudolf II's alchemists lived here is indeed exciting, but untrue. Only in the 19th century did people rediscover Golden Lane's magical atmosphere, with some artists dwelling here at the start of the 20th century. The most popular of them, Franz Kafka, rented house no. 22 in 1916-17. Architect Pavel Janák authored reconstruction of the homes on Golden Lane in 1952-55. Today this area is explicitly a tourist attraction, and various types of souvenirs are sold in the diminutive houses. Walking along the defense corridor, you may enter house no. 24. It has small loophole windows and is a part of the wall. Today it holds an exhibit of old military weaponry and hardware.

Bridges

6 Charles Bridge
50°5'11.53"N, 14°24'40.58"E

Besides Hradčany district, Charles Bridge is the Prague icon most frequently used in guides and brochures attracting tourists to the capital city. Visitors are sure to take plenty pictures of it while here in Prague. It's stood here for ages, longer than all other Prague bridges, connecting Old Town with the Lesser Side. But it wasn't the first stone bridge here. After a 10th-century wooden bridge came the stone Judith Bridge, built around 1170 by Vladislav II. But the bridge and the city were and still are threatened by flooding. Judith Bridge finally succumbed to a flood in 1342. Charles IV commissioned a new bridge, first called Stone or Prague Bridge, to stand beside the remains of the older one in 1357. It came to be known as Charles Bridge only in the 19th century. Petr Parléř led construction of the sandstone block bridge (around 520 m long, 10 m wide). Bridge towers stand like bookends on both ends – one in Old Town and two on the Lesser Side. But the thirty statues and sculptures found all along both sides complete the bridge's appearance and make it a unique work of art unlike any other on earth. Most of them were created in 1683–1714 by the day's great sculptors, the most famous of which were Matyáš Bernard Braun, Jan Brokof and his sons Michal Jan and Ferdinand Maxmilián. St. John of Nepomuk's statue is the oldest and is the only one made out of bronze Some original works were destroyed by floods and replaced with others, mainly in the 19th century.

7 Čech Bridge
⊕ 50°5'35.671"N, 14°25'1.251"E

Svatopluk Čech Bridge became part of the grand building of the modern metropolis in relation to the demolition of the erstwhile Jewish Town. It was built in 1905–08 as an extension of Pařížská street by design of architect Jan Koula. This green arch bridge with Art Nouveau elements spans the Vltava at a relatively narrow point, so its length of 169 meters makes it Prague's shortest bridge.

It measures 16 meters in width. The bridge holds within the mains for water, gas and electricity. It boasts rich sculpting decoration (on high columns four figures of Victorias with gilded wings, bronze statues of torchbearers and six-headed Hydra with the emblems of Prague), and even wrought iron railing and arches.

8 Hlávka Bridge
50°5'44.98"N, 14°26'13.44"E

This bridge, named after renowned builder and missionary Josef Hlávka, is Prague's only bridge bearing its original name. It has other unique features – it was the first to be built out of concrete in Prague or anywhere else in the republic. Of course, this came after reconstruction in 1958–62. Part of the structure from 1908–10 was built from iron by design of Mečislav Petrů, and the second part from 1910–12 was built from concrete by designers František Mencl and Pavel Janák. On the left bridgehead stands the statue *Work* and *Humanity* by Jan Štursa. The planned monument to Josef Hlávka never came to fruition.

Quarters and Squares

9 Old Town Square
⌖ 50°5'14.72"N, 14°25'15.32"E

The attribute "the most" is befitting for Old Town Square in many ways. It is Prague's most beautiful and Old Town's oldest and most important square, once with the city's liveliest market. It is surrounded by Romanesque and Gothic houses. It was part of the Royal Route and has seen many great historic events. Today people gather during political, cultural and sports events. The town hall stood here by the 14th century as did Old Town's main Church of Our Lady before Týn. Old Town Hall is a group of several buildings with a prismatic tower. The Neo-Gothic wing burnt down in May of 1945, and the tower and Astronomical Clock also suffered heavy damage. Today its historic halls and chapel are accessible. You'll go by glass elevator up to the tower walkway to get a grand view of the city. The other areas hold exhibits, and weddings are held in the wedding hall. Across the square towards Týn Church stand two important buildings – the House at the Stone Bell and Kinský Palace. The first hides a lovely Gothic home with a stone bell on the corner under the Baroque shell, founded in the second half of the 13th century. It got its original appearance after complex reconstruction in the 1960s and 1970s. This was probably the palace of Eliška Přemyslidna, mother of Charles IV. According to the Zbraslav chronicles, Charles IV lived here after returning to Bohemia. Exhibits and concerts are held inside. The Kinský Palace, another of today's galleries, stands right beside it. Its appearance came during last modifications in the first half of the 19th century. The first Nobel Peace Prize laureate, Berta Suttnerová-Kinská, was born here in 1843 to the family of its owners. The building later held the German gymnasium, attended by Franz Kafka, whose father had a ground-floor shop here. Gottwald's speech here from the palace balcony on February 25, 1948, marked the start of 40 years of communist rule. The Master Jan Hus is one of the most famous Czechs. A monument to him was unveiled unofficially and without permission at this spot in 1915 to mark 500 years since his execution in Constance. Ladislav Šaloun was the author of this bronze Secession sculpture on stone pedestal.

10 Josefov
⊕ 50°5'25.87"N, 14°25'6.00"E

Josefov, or Jewish Town, is more closely related to the fortunes and fates of Prague's Jewish community than all other localities. Today it is one of the most visited places in the Czech Republic. Like others European cities at the end of the 19th century, Prague wanted to rid itself of narrow, crooked medieval streets, and build modern, big-city boulevards with ostentatious homes. So a plan was formed to demolish Josefov, justified by the claim of unsatisfactory hygienic conditions, multiple illnesses, high mortality rate, overpopulation or lack of drinking water. Several hundred homes were razed. Today's Pařížská street became its main boulevard lined by Neo-Baroque and Secession homes. Other streets were widened (such as Kaprova, Maislova, and Dušní). The only things remaining from the old development were the town hall, Jewish cemetery and six synagogues – the Old-New, Klausen, Maisel, Pinkas, Spanish and High synagogues. The Old-New Synagogue, a two-nave Gothic structure, is Europe's oldest preserved synagogue. Services are still regularly held in this 13th-century synagogue. The High Synagogue is also still used as a prayer hall. The other mentioned synagogues hold exhibits of the Jewish Museum representing the history of Jews in Bohemia and Moravia, Jewish traditions, customs, holidays and everyday life. The Pinkas Synagogue exhibits children's drawings from Terezín. Its walls bear the names of the nearly 80,000 names of Czech Jews murdered during the holocaust. The Old Jewish Cemetery attracts visitors from around the world for its history, preserved state and singular atmosphere. It was founded in the first half of the 15th century, functioning until 1787, when a ban came on burials within inhabited parts of cities. Its preserved 12,000 gravestones form amazing groups, shadowed by many tall trees. But there are actually many more graves here, because for lack of space people were buried on top of one another literally forming stacks of graves per spot. This caused older gravestones to be pushed up to higher layers, so they appear beside the newer ones. The most famous personality buried here is Rabbi Jehuda Liwa ben Becalel, also known as Rabbi Löw, religious scholar, philosopher and teacher, related with the legend of the creation of an animate being – the Golem of Prague.

11 Old Jewish Cemetery
⊕ 50°5'22.69"N, 14°25'1.60"E

During the great demolition of Prague's Josefov at the turn of the 20th century, the Jewish Town retained precious few monuments – six synagogues, the town hall and the Old Jewish Cemetery, the latter of which attracts visitors from around the world for its history, preserved state and captivating atmosphere. Though founded in the first half of the 15th century, it wasn't Prague's oldest cemetery. It functioned until 1787, when burials were banned within inhabited parts of cities. The cemetery space grew through purchases of surrounding plots. The cemetery was walled in 1911. Its preserved 12,000 gravestones form amazing groups, shadowed by many tall trees. The oldest monument is from 1439 and honors the scholar and poet Avigdor Karo. But there are actually many more graves here, because for lack of space people were buried on top of one another literally forming stacks of graves per spot, allegedly up to a dozen in certainly places. This caused older gravestones to be pushed up to higher layers, so they appear beside the newer ones. It even captures the actual development of several architectural styles. From the epitaphs and sculptural symbols, besides names and dates, there is much more to read about the deceased, e.g. their origin, personal qualities or profession. The most famous figure buried here is Rabbi Jehuda Liwa ben Becalel, also known as Rabbi Löw or the Prague Maharal, a religious scholar, philosopher and teacher (around 1525–1609). Since the 19th century, his persona has been bound to the legend of the creation of an artificial being – the Golem of Prague. Also lying here are the famous Primate of the Jewish Town and missionary Mordechaj Maisel (1528–1601), and a series of others.

12 Wenceslas Square
 50°4'54.90"N, 14°25'35.97"E

Horse Market, renamed Václavské náměstí ("Wenceslas Square"), is the recognized center of not just New Town, but all of Prague. Its best-known symbol is the equestrian statue of St. Wenceslas, patron saint of the Czech lands. It's stood on a high base in the square's upper corner below the National Museum since 1913. Four Czech saints surround Prince Wenceslas – St. Ludmila, St. Agnes of Bohemia, St. Adalbert and St. Procopius. Josef Václav Myslbek created the monument's design in 1890-94. The statue has long served as a landmark and meeting place that's very easy to find. Ostentatious buildings lining both sides of the square replaced older structures in the latter-19th and 20th centuries. Palaces grew here, as well as banks, hotels and department stores in various architectural styles. Three buildings (a food emporium, house of fashion and Hotel Jalta) were built in the 1950s where buildings bombed out in 1945 had stood. Many structures are exceptionally valuable. Architect Antonín Wiehl built the Wiehl House (no. 34, today the Academia publishing company seat) by his own design. The Neo-Renaissance building is richly decorated with ornamental and figural historically-themed sgraffito. The so-called Peterka House (no. 12, today Salamander) is an early Kotěra Secession building from 1899. The functionalist Baťa department store with full glass façade built in 1927–29, based on design by Ludvík Kysela, was one of the most modern department stores of its time.

13 Charles Square
⊕ 50°4'32.96"N, 14°25'11.85"E

Large cities always have several squares. The same is true in Prague. "Charles Square", Prague's largest, is found in New Town from the period of its founding by Charles IV. It has held various names over the times; it was called Cattle Market from the 15th century, as it was just that, a cattle market. It wasn't named after its founder until the mid-19th century. The first park landscaping of this sprawling area came later that century thanks to Count Karel Chotek. František Thomayer, then director of Prague Gardens and Parks, consolidated the appearance of both parts and planted rows of trees in 1884-85. This green square holds a series of statues (of Vítězslav Hálek, Eliška Krásnohorská, Karolína Světlá and other important personalities), and three fountains. Several impressive buildings stand around the square. At the northern side is the New Town Hall from the mid-14th century with mid-15th century tower. It saw Renaissance and later Classicist restoration. Then reconstruction in 1904–05 gave it back its mid-16th century Renaissance appearance. Today the tower and other areas holding occasional exhibits are accessible. The opposite end of the square features the mysterious Faust Home, originally Gothic, later restored in Renaissance and Baroque styles. One of its most famous owners was Edward Kelly, an alchemist to Rudolf II. But another of its owners from the Mladota family did perform physical and chemical experiments, hence the relationship between Dr. Faust and this house. The house was heavily damaged by Allied bombing in February, 1945. Today it is a part of a faculty hospital. Czech Technical University in Prague is the oldest university of its type in Europe, founded in 1707 but under a different name. After it split into Czech and German parts in 1869, the Czech school needed its own building. A project by architect Ignác Ullmann was chosen in 1871 – a massive Neo-Renaissance structure, whose façade faces Karlovo náměstí. The allegorical statues *Work and Science* (by Antonín Popp) embellish the main entrance, while Myslbek's sculptures of geniuses hang over the third floor windows. But other planned wings were never built.

14. Vyšehrad Cemetery and Slavín

50°3'52.70"N, 14°25'4.52"E

Prague's Vyšehrad district dates back to the oldest history of the city and the Czech lands. A seat was founded above a steep cliff over the Vltava. It was an age-old symbol of Czech statehood in the days of the first princes in the 10th and 11th centuries. Vyšehrad, walled in on almost all sides, is made up of several buildings, parks, a cemetery and playground. The grounds are entered by three gates. Interesting views of Prague are offered from several points, especially of the Vltava river valley. Its grand monuments include the 11th-century Rotunda of St. Martin, the Church of SS Peter and Paul, and cemetery. The Church of SS Peter and Paul at Vyšehrad dominates the grounds, founded back in the latter-11th century. But its appearance comes from its last alteration in 1903. This Romanesque capitulary basilica has seen Gothic, Renaissance and Baroque phases, up to Neo-Gothicism. Vyšehrad's cliff with slender twin towers forms one of Prague's most typical panoramas. Its cemetery holds about 600 of the nation's greatest personalities from many fields, especially writers, poets, scientists, painters, sculptors, architects, actors, singers, composers, doctors and politicians. The main cemetery path leads to Slavín (Pantheon), the common tomb of the Czech nation's greats. Its motto reads: *"Though dead, they still speak"*.

15 Olšany Cemetery
◈ 50°4'49.70"N, 14°27'59.50"E

The origin of Prague's biggest graveyard, actually a complex of fourteen graveyards 50 ha in size, is linked to a plague epidemic of 1679. At the time, its owner sold the former garden to Prague's Old Town as a place to bury the victims of this deadly disease. The location served the same purpose after yet another plague epidemic in 1715–16. The year 1682 saw completion of the Chapel of St. Roch, St. Sebastian and St. Rosalia, protectors from plague. It transformed into the parish Church of the Exaltation in the first half of the 19th century. As of the ban on burying in the center of town issued by Joseph II in 1786, it changed from a plague cemetery to a public cemetery. As the city grew, so did this place of final rest of its residents residing on the Vltava's right bank. By today, an alleged two million people have been buried here. However, they are far from all being Praguers; they come from various parts of our country and abroad – war dead from the Battle of Dresden of 1813, fallen Czech legionnaires, Russian soldiers from both World Wars, soldiers from Commonwealth nations or Prague Uprising victims. In the part set off for Orthodox and Greek Catholics stands the Russian Orthodox Temple of the Dormition of the Most Holy Theotokos from 1924–25. The Olšany Cemetery's Jewish part emerged in 1890 after the ban on burying at the Žižkov Jewish Cemetery, whose small part still remains by the television tower. The most famous personality buried here is Franz Kafka, epitaphs from many gravestones are symbolically reminiscent of the victims of the Holocaust, though in reality none are buried here. Since Olšany Cemetery contains many artistically priceless examples of Czech funerary sculptures of the 18th-20th century, it has been inscribed as a protected monument.

Chateaux and Summer Palaces

16 Troja Chateau
50°6'59.10"N, 14°24'46.34"E

Many noble seats rose around Prague in the 17th century. The Baroque Troja chateau is one of the most important. Count Václav Vojtěch of Šternberk had it built as a family summer residence along the Vltava. Building began in 1679 based on design by Giovanni Domenico Orsi. Architect and painter Jean Baptiste Mathey continued in his work a few years later, gathering inspiration from Roman country villas. Italian, German and Dutch masters embellished it with sculptures and paintings. The main hall's walls and ceiling feature frescoes celebrating the Habsburg family, especially Austrian victory over Turkey in 1863. Today it's used as a concert hall. Other areas are also richly decorated with frescoes.

The chateau is surrounded by a sprawling French garden, connected by a grandiose double staircase adorned with statues of the gods of antiquity battling Titans. Today the chateau holds a permanent exhibit called Eternal Summer in a Roman Villa, containing several parts. The Architecture and Decoration of Troja section presents the history of this structure, and the part From the Noble Residences shows historical images of dogs, horses and other animals. City Gallery Prague's picture gallery holds exhibits of important works of Czech 19th-century painting. And finally in the Chinese chambers with oriental furniture, you'll see Chinese landscape wall paintings. Other area hold occasional exhibitions.

17 Governor's Summer Palace in Stromovka
50°6'16.74"N, 14°24'51.07"E

The royal preserve, usually referred to as Stromovka, is one of Prague's loveliest and greatest parks, spreading out over around 95 hectares. But it suffered serious damage in the flood of 2002, and has since undergone extensive alterations. On its southern edge at its highest point stands the building of the Governor's Summer Palace, because it was used as a summer residence of royal governors after its restoration that had commenced in 1804. Its appearance comes from this time. Also the preserve was opened to the public at the time. But the history of the residence and preserve goes back much farther, probably to the time of Přemysl Otakar II, when a hunting fortress was probably built here. A Gothic building was built here in 1495-1502 at its spot. Emperor Rudolf II has this (and many other buildings) redesigned in Renaissance style at the end of the 16th century. He had a large, no longer existing pond built, fed from the Vltava by the 1,102-meter long "Rudolf's tunnel" drilled underneath Letná. It is an important technical monument but is not open to the public. It's also not normally possible to enter the summer palace, although its valuable interior has been preserved. That's because it houses the periodicals department of the National Museum, with its work station, study and depository. One day a week has been determined for researchers. You can at least get to the terrace, from where you'll enjoy a spectacular view of Prague and a 17th-century sun dial.

18 Hvězda Summer Residence
50°5'0.24"N, 14°19'34.38"E

Educated and art-loving Archduke Ferdinand of Tyrol was the vice-regent of Prague in 1547–67. He decided to build a summer residence by his own design in the Břevnov preserve. Its six-sided star ground plan is highly unusual, but comes from principles of which Ferdinand was a follower – harmony, symmetry, symbolism of numbers and the heliocentric arrangement of space. The star also symbolizes the birth of Jesus Christ. The Renaissance structure was built in 1555-56, led by builders of Italian descent, Giovanni Mario Aostalli and Giovanni Lucchese.

The ground floor was given lovely stucco decoration with themes of antiquity. The 3rd-floor banquet hall has an interesting mosaic floor formed by glazed tiles. The Battle of White Mountain, fought nearby the summer residence, marked a period of decline for this structure. Major yet sensitive reconstruction based on design of architect Pavel Janák took place in 1949-51. Then the Alois Jirásek Museum was opened, followed by the Mikoláš Aleš Museum. Further reconstruction occurred in 1996-2004, and the Hvězda National Cultural Monument has welcomed visitors ever since. The basement areas hold a model of the Battle of White Mountain complete with little tin soldiers. The permanent exhibit called *Past and Present* familiarizes visitors with the architectural development of the summer residence and its history. Second-floor exhibits are normally dedicated to literature, displaying collections of the Museum of Czech Literature. The building is also the venue for concerts, lectures and other social events.

19 Kinský Summer Palace
50°4'36.93"N, 14°23'55.27"E

The grounds on the Smíchov side of Petřín Hill belonged to Princess Růžena Kinská by the end of the 18th century, who intended to plant a fruit orchard. But her son Rudolf had other plans. English-type parks imitating nature had become fashionable in the first half of the 19th century, as had Classicist chateaux. And that's the design Rudolf Kinský achieved. The beautiful garden designed by František Höhnel was created in 1825, and the summer palace was built in 1827-31, designed by Viennese architect, Heinrich Koch. The garden with pond, waterfall and greenhouse was accessible for a fee twice a week, and interest was great. Other buildings included a coach house, a house for its employees, etc. Collections began to appear in the chateau in 1902, created during the World Jubilee Exhibition of 1891 and the Czech National Exhibition of 1895. The National History Museum functioned here until 1986. But the building was is such bad state it had to be vacated, leaving its fate in question. The National Museum was finally chosen to assume control over it, which it did in 1999, and the wonderfully reconstructed building was reopened to the public in 2005. Examples of folk costumes, customs, crafts, folk art and the way of life over the ecclesiastical year are found upstairs in the museum known as Musaion. Occasional exhibits are held on the ground floor, and it holds several practically usable workshops. Public lectures, workshops and technical folklore symposia are held in the hall.

20 Bertramka

◇ 50°4'13.66"N, 14°23'42.06"E

Several estates arose on the hills of today's Smíchov in the 16th century, amongst them the so-called Bertramka. Operatic singer Josefína Dušková and her husband, musical composer and pianist František Xaver Dušek, bought it in 1784 and owned it for 15 years. Thanks to them, this Classicist villa gained fame as a place where Wolfgang Amadeus Mozart found sanctuary during trips to Prague. He completed his opera Don Giovanni here, which premiered on October 29, 1787. It was very popular amongst Praguers, and in 1791, shortly before his death, Mozart presented his opera La clemenza di Tito upon the crowning of Emperor Leopold II as Czech King. Lambert Popelka gained Bertramka in 1838. He was a great admirer of Mozart's music. His son even made rooms public where Mozart allegedly dwelled, and he collected mementoes to the famous composer. Memorial celebrations were held here to mark the 100th anniversary of Don Giovanni's premiere. The last private owner left the estate in 1925 to the foundation named Mozarteum, which sold it to Prague's Mozart Community in 1929. Classical music concerts are held here regularly in the garden in the summer and in the sala terrena during inclement weather.

Palaces

21 Archbishop's Palace
✣ 50°5'24.59"N, 14°23'50.96"E

Emperor Charles IV founded the Czech archbishopric in 1344. The archbishop's seat changed many times over centuries, whereas today's seat on the square Hradčanské náměstí has been used since 1561. This palace has been restored several times thereafter. Architect Jean Baptista Mathey designed it in early Baroque fashion in the latter-17th century. Its Rococo appearance came during reconstruction in 1764-65 under Archbishop Antonín Petr Příchovský, whose distinctive coat-of-arms is found in the central buttress. The allegoric figures Bravery and Lenience hang above it. The archbishop entrusted this work to meaningful Czech architect, Jan Josef Wirch. He gave the palace side wings and a fourth floor. He also gave the façade its famous Rococo appearance. The entire complex runs all the way to Deer Moat. Ignác František Platzer authored the sculpture embellishment, but his works were replaced at the end of the 19th century with copies by Čeněk Vosmík. The palace holds highly valuable interiors. It contains wood carving work, rich stucco work, period furniture, rare chandeliers, crystal and porcelain. Its amazing representation halls include Trophy Hall with a cycle of nine French tapestries from the mid-18th century, which capture so-called New India, and a dining room with portraits of Prague archbishops. The latest, this time very thorough and costly repair of the palace came in 1995-98. The garden, designed by architect František J. Thomayer, was reconstructed in 2000, but is not open to the public.

22 Wallenstein Palace
50°5'24.87"N, 14°24'23.89"E

PALACES

Building also flourished after the Battle of White Mountain and during the Thirty Years War, because it's possible to profit from war. This was the case of the most distinctive figure of this period – Albrecht von Wallenstein (Valdštejn). With intrinsic disregard he bought up more than twenty homes, several gardens and a brick works, and ambitiously set out to match the emperor and compete with Prague Castle itself by building his monumental Prague seat on these grounds. Construction of Wallenstein Palace by design of Andrea Spezza started in 1624. It is Prague's first and largest Baroque structure. A number of important Italian builders and artists worked on it. The entire complex of three-storey palace and two-storey administrative and out-buildings center around extraordinary gardens and five courtyards. Accessible from the metro exit or from Valdštejnská street, the former Riding Hall is today a sought-after gallery featuring large, important exhibits. The representative palace interiors are open on weekends. Wallenstein Gardens are also open from April till the end of October, with precious sala terrena, grotto and bronze sculptures of ancient gods. The Swedes took the originals by Adrian de Vries in 1648 as war booty, so 19th century copies stand in the garden. Summer visitors enjoy pleasant strolls here and can sometimes see theater presentations and concerts.

23 Černín Palace

◊ 50°5'19.59"N, 14°23'24.68"E

This massive palace's façade segmented by thirty semi-columns faces the square Loretánské náměstí. Its construction started in 1669 for a very rich Imperial diplomat, Count Humprecht Jan Czernin of Chudenice. Francesco Caratti became the main architect, but over the decades the palace saw many popular architects, stone masons, plasterers, painters and sculptors. But the family had to relinquish their property after no longer having revenue to finance its expensive administration and maintenance. History had a way of affecting the fates of the palace, mostly in unfavorable terms, like in 1742 when French and Bavarian forces destroyed it, followed by Prussians in 1757. The Czernins left it at the end of the 18th century. It then housed a hospital, workshops, storage areas, and later Prague's poor. The Austrian government, its new owners, turned it into barracks in 1848, leading to damage to its interiors and the garden. It was decided upon the creation of Czechoslovakia that the palace would house the Ministry of Foreign Affairs, but it first had to be fully reconstructed (1928-34). Architect Pavel Janák sensitively restored the palace to its original likeness based on Caratti's rediscovered blueprints. It also received the so-called Janák wing, an administrative building still used as an office today. Edvard Beneš became the first foreign minister to work here. The "Reichsprotektor" ruled from here during WWII, followed by the return of the Czechoslovak Ministry of Foreign Affairs. Neither the palace nor the garden, whose fate has remained intertwined with the palace, is publicly accessible.

24 Schwarzenberg Palace
50°5'20.43"N, 14°23'48.43"E

Several grandiose palaces stand near Prague Castle, long belonging to important noble families. The Renaissance Schwarzenberg Palace is one whose black and white Venetian and Northern Italy-style sgraffito immediately attracts attention when viewing the Hradčany panorama. Italian and Czech elements are combined in this structure, the result of which is a lovely example of the so-called Bohemian Renaissance. The younger Jan of Lobkowicz had this impressive seat built in 1545-67 upon grounds where several buildings had burnt down. He entrusted its building to Agostin Galli, who built the three-wing palace with high gables and court of honor. Painted coffered ceilings have been preserved within. But the Lobkowicz family did not own the palace for long, because Emperor Rudolf II despised the next owner Jiří of Lobkowicz and confiscated his property. The last in the series of noble families to whom this seat belonged were the Schwarzenbergs as of 1719. They had it repaired and had new residential areas built. After the western gable came crashing down in 1870, Josef Schulz repaired it and restored the sgraffito. This was restored several times thereafter. It now belongs to the National Gallery, which has installed here an extensive, very interesting exhibit on the Baroque Period in Bohemia, presenting Baroque sculpture, painting and artistic craftsmanship. It has programs for children and various interest groups. Visitors may admire the preserved painted ceilings in some third-floor halls.

25 Lobkowicz Palace
⌖ 50°5'13.58"N, 14°23'53.12"E

The Lesser Side's Lobkowicz Palace has been the seat of the Federal Republic of Germany since 1971. František Karel Přehořovský of Kvasejovice gained the vineyards with the house At the Three Musketeers at the foot of Petřín Hill at the start of the 17th century. He had built here a High Baroque three-winged palace designed by architect Giovanni Battista Alliprandi, one of Prague's loveliest and most valuable. In 1753 it came under ownership of the Lobkowicz family, who stayed here until 1927. It got its current appearance by design of Ignác Jan Palliardi after a fire in 1768. Another floor was added at the time. The façade facing the terraced garden forms a sala terrena with rich stucco adornment. This is also characteristic of the palace. The vestibule and ground-floor halls are covered by valuable frescoes by Jan Jakub Steinfels. The state bought the palace in 1927. For years various offices and scientific institutions resided here. It became an embassy after WWII. In 1989, thousands of German Democratic Republic's citizens request asylum here and the possibility to move to the Federal Republic of Germany. The situation was very drastic. People even with small children were climbing over the fence to get in, sleeping in tents in the garden, which was badly devastated. The symbol of these events stands in the garden – a bronze statue by David Černý named Quo vadis – a Trabant automobile standing on four high legs. Hundreds of owners of these vehicles left them behind in Prague.

Monasteries

26 St. Agnes of Bohemia Convent
⊕ 50°5′32.61″N, 14°25′26.11″E

A National Cultural Monument stands in the Prague area of na Františku, said to be Bohemia's oldest Gothic complex. It is the St. Agnes of Bohemia Convent, founded by King Wenceslas I. The idea came from his sister Agnes Přemyslid, who brought in the Order of Poor Clares and became the convent's first abbess. The convent grounds are quite complex and highly advanced in terms of 13th-century architecture. It was then formed of two institutions – the Poor Clares convent and neighboring Minorite monastery. The early Gothic, two-nave St. Francis Church was added to the two-storey convent in 1240. The Minorites took over this church and a new one was built for the Poor Clares. The Church of the Holy Saviour was added in 1270-80. Royal tombstones are found in the choir, such as that of St. Wenceslas I. The convent was abandoned after the Hussite Wars and fell to ruin; St. Francis Church's vault even caved in. It again served its purpose in the 16th and 17th centuries, but like many it was closed under Joseph II. Prague's poor settled within. The complex was to be razed at the end of the 19th century. Luckily this did not occur. Archeological research was eventually performed and completed in 1986 over several phases with long breaks in reconstruction. The St. Francis Church was given a new roof and had its concert hall modified, and the first exhibit of the National Gallery was opened in 1980. Today the convent holds an old art collection of the National Gallery called Medieval Art in Bohemia and Central Europe.

27 Strahov Monastery
50°5'10.46"N, 14°23'23.10"E

MONASTERIES

The National Cultural Heritage Monument Strahov Monastery is the country's oldest Premonstrate monastery. Prince (later King) Vladislav II founded it in 1140 at the urging of Olomouc Bishop Jindřich Zdík. Thus the allegedly largest Romanesque structure in Bohemia stood by 1182 at a spot with a stunning view of Prague and Prague Castle. Archeological research in the 1950s uncovered preserved Romanesque elements, which disappeared however in the course of the many centuries of complex building development of the monastery and the Church of the Assumption. The complex's Baroque appearance is the result of mainly 18th-century modifications on which the period's great architects, builders and artists worked. The church's greatest events were gaining the remains of St. Norbert, the order's founder, and its raising to a minor basilica by Pope John Paul II in 1992. The library has been important throughout the monastery's history. Today it has amassed a total of 200,000 books, amongst which are many old manuscripts and original printings. The Theological Hall, created in 1671 for the rarest specimens, boasts rich stucco embellishment and amazing ceiling frescoes. After its completion, the library was expanded to include the Classicist Philosophical Hall. Strahov's public gallery holds valuable Czech and European art collections from the Gothic and other periods. Visitors may explore the cloisters, Chapter Hall, the winter and summer refectories or the Romanesque alls. The monastery is also proud to have reopened its restored brewery, with fresh brewed beer and a lovely restaurant.

28 Břevnov Monastery
◆ 50°5'4.26"N, 14°21'24.30"E

The monastery in Břevnov is Bohemia's oldest male monastery. It was founded in 993 by St Adalbert, Prague's second bishop from the Slavník family, and the Přemyslid Prince Boleslaus II "the Pious". Legend has it that they met above a well, the source of the Brusnice brook, where the Vojtěška summer house with chapel now stands. A pre-Romanesque crypt remains of the original monastery, discovered during 1960s archeological research under the choir of the Church of St. Margaret. The building has been restored several times, and suffered both the Hussite Wars and the Thirty Years War. New life had to wait until the 18th century. A high-Baroque structure was built in 1708-45 by design of Kryštof and Kilián Ignác Dientzenhofer. A courtyard opens up behind the entrance gate where the Church of St. Margaret stands, elevated by Pope Pious XII to a minor basilica – a church under special papal protection. The monastery's single-nave interior is richly embellished with valuable wall and ceiling paintings. The author of the altar paintings is Petr Brandl, and Matouš Václav Jäckel created the sculptures along the sides of the altars. The convent and prelature are of high architectural importance, especially the so-called Theresian Hall, the most valuable part of the prelature named after Empress Maria Theresa upon her visit here in 1753. The garden, also a part of the complex, also has a Baroque layout. The monastery became famous in 1995 when Pope John Paul II met here with Czech friars.

Churches

29 Church of Our Lady before Týn
✧ 50°5′15.63″N, 14°25′21.80″E

Týn Church is one of the awe-inspiring architectural wonders on Old Town Square, one of Prague's loveliest locations. It was founded in the mid-14th century – a period of major building expansion in Prague initiated by Emperor Charles IV. But it seemed the work was in no hurry; when the Hussite Wars erupted it still lacked a roof but was functioning as a church. Certain venerable reforming evangelists preached here at the time. In 1427, the lone Prague Hussite Archbishop Jan Rokycana became the local rector, and was later laid to rest here. Týn Church was completed under King George of Poděbrady, who saw to building the 80-meter north tower. Its south tower however wasn't built until the next century. The historic turmoil of the nation was also seen in the church's gable – the 15th century statue of George of Poděbrady and his great gilded chalice was replaced by a statue of the Madonna in the 17th century. Her halo comes from that original gold. The interior's valuable works of art include those of Gothic, Renaissance and Baroque periods, such as the pewter Gothic font, the Gothic canopy and Týn Madonna, Karel Škréta's early Baroque altarpieces over the main altar or the embellishment of the side altars by other great artists. Of its many preserved tombstones, the most popular belongs to Tycho Brahe, Rudolf II's Danish astronomer. Prague's oldest pipe organ makes Týn all the more valuable. The church also holds services, and is used as a concert hall and tourist attention.

30 St. Nicholas Church (Lesser Side)
⊕ 50°5'16.51"N, 14°24'11.74"E

Just as the Týn Church towers are a quintessential image of Old Town, the St. Nicholas Church towers are an indelible feature of the Lesser Side. This church standing right in this district's center is considered a pinnacle of Baroque architecture. The Prague Jesuits were responsible for its founding. In the 17th century, they gradually obtained certain buildings and grounds in this area. They built here a professional home and gymnasium, and began in 1703 to build a new church based on design by Kryštof Dientzenhofer. The first part of the structure was consecrated in 1711 – the facade, nave and chapel. The architect's son Kilián Ignác Dientzenhofer continued building it after his death, creating an utterly different cupola than his father had conceived. This monumental cupola measures 70 meters from the outside and 50 meters on the inside. František Xaver Palko adorned it with a fresco of the Celebration of the Holy Trinity. But its interior holds many more frescoes, aside from the mentioned artist and his colleagues; another important creator was Johann Kracker of Vienna. Other paintings by Karel Škréta are also priceless like his Crucifixion in the Chapel of St. Barbara. Its fifty or so statues were created in the workshop of Ignác František Platzer. The belfry, completed by Anselmo Lurago after its author's death, was built along with the church. Both towers are the same height. The reconstructed tower was opened to the public in the late 1990s. People may ascend the 215 stairs to a Prague bell exhibit.

31 Church of Our Lady of Victory (Carmelite)
50°4'33.56"N, 14°19'17.98"E

This church from 1611–13, originally concentrated as the Most Holy Trinity Church, belonged to German Lutherans. It happens to be the oldest Baroque structure in Prague, a first in architectural history here. Its architect was most likely Giovanni Maria Filippi. After the Battle of White Mountain and consequent recatholization of the lands, the Discalced Carmelites received it as a gift from Emperor Ferdinand II. After many twists and turns, the church eventually returned to the hands of the Carmelites. The greatest magnet for church visitors is the wax statuette of the Infant Jesus of Prague, brought here from Spain in the mid-16th century. Polyxena von Lobkowicz donated it to the church. This Infant Jesus, beloved worldwide, wears different clothing during various church holidays, and has several dozen little outfits in his wardrobe. Beneath the church is a crypt closed to the public with the mummified bodies of monks.

32 Church of St. Wenceslas of Smíchov
50°4'24.20"N, 14°24'16.86"E

Smíchov's new social status in the latter-19th century gave rise to the building of a church consecrated to St. Wenceslas. The number of citizens grew sharply, and the small village gradually became a city of 25,000 inhabitants by 1880. This was because of ever-expanding industry, especially textile and iron manufacture. The diminutive Church of St. Philip and Jacob that stood at today's square Arbesovo náměstí was razed, and replaced in 1881 by a much larger capacity church. Builders Jan Linhart and Václav Milde led construction that finished in 1885 based on design by architect Antonín Barvitius. Unfortunately to make room, one of the wings called Portheimka had to be demolished – once the summer seat of Kilián Ignác Dientzenhofer. Thus was formed a Neo-Renaissance three-nave basilica with two 50-meter high towers with copper sheet roofing. The contrast between stone and fair-faced brick was used for its exterior appearance. On the relief above the main nave's portal hangs the image of St. Wenceslas and angels. The interior embellishing was entrusted to the day's most sought-after artists. One example is the mosaic in the main apse illustrating Christ surrounded by saints, especially Czech ones – Wenceslas, Ludmila, Procopius and Adalbert. Josef Trenkwald designed it. Čeněk Vosmík authored the large group of statues on the main altar and others. The wooden, polychrome cassette ceiling beckons one's attention upon entering. The church holds regular services and occasionally even concerts.

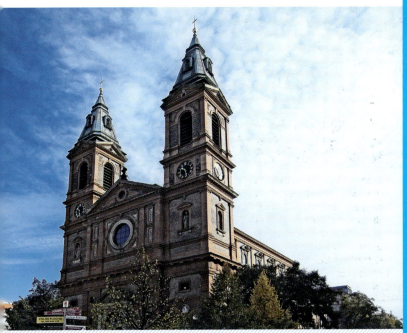

33 Church of the Sacred Heart
50°4'40.90"N, 14°27'2.53"E

A major construction boom erupted across Czechoslovakia following its creation. The capacity of the Vinohrady parish Church of St. Ludmila at today's square náměstí Míru no longer sufficed, so the decision came to build another church, for which city officials opened a tender in 1919. There were 31 applicants, but eventually at the insistence of some Czech architects, the job was offered to Slovenian architect Josip Plečnik, already famous here for his work remodeling Prague Castle. He wasn't actually in the tender, but finally assumed the task after some reluctance. The church was built in 1928–32. The entirely different and ultramodern building inspired by old Christian basilicas is 38 meters long and 26 meters wide. Its cassette ceiling reaches a height of 13 meters. The belfry, topped by a 4-meter cross, is 42 meters high and is relatively wide. The window, reminiscent in size and shape to the rosace of Gothic churches, was eventually given a clock. The façade is very original, made from twice-fired brick combined with lighter stone blocks. This combination and its arrangement are reminiscent of Royal ermine, which is symbolic both in regards to the church's consecration and to the square named after King George Poděbrady and found in the royal area of Královské Vinohrady. The church lacks a pulpit; by the white marble altar you'll see a sculpture of Christ and six gigantic Czech saints.

Modern Architecture

34 Villa Bílek

50°5'42.61"N, 14°24'30.13"E

František Bílek (1872–1941) was an architect, painter, graphic artists, illustrator and mystic. He designed for himself and his family an utterly unique villa with studio in 1910, a pearl of the Czech Secession. He authored not just the villa but also its entire furnishing to the last detail, even including hot-air heating. He commissioned builder Antonín Hulán, who completed his task in 1911. The entire concept was derived from an artistic view of the world and art. The ground plan symbolizes the trace of a scythe in a field of grain; its stone columns separating fair-faced brickwork are stylized wheat heads, the flat roof also resembles a field, the first of its kind in Prague. This symbolism is even maintained in the interior, like the carved wooden doors, cabinets and chairs or the metal door handles. The main area in this villa is its studio, connected to other rooms and the garden. All of the emanated from the yearning to form a so-called Gesamktunstwerk, a complete work of art. After Bílek's death, his studio was opened to the public. In 1963, the artist's wife dedicated the house to the City of Prague, and the City Gallery Prague became its caretaker. The aim to build a monument wasn't fulfilled until 1993. The exhibit thus includes the studio of František Bílek, living quarters, the Otokar Březina room, and statues, drawings and graphics are displayed.

35 Koruna Palace
◈ 50°5′3.49″N, 14°25′27.88″E

In 1911, where Wenceslas Square meets the street Na Příkopě, several old structures from the times of founding New Town by Charles IV were razed to make room for new, modern buildings. The First Czech General Corporation life insurance agency built a late Secession palace here with five-above ground and two underground floors in 1911-12. Architect Antonín Pfeiffer and builder Matěj Blecha took part in its design and implementation. At this time a reinforced concrete skeleton frame came into fashion. This advanced design was applied here too. Its corner tower is the entire structure's most expressive feature, underneath which stand allegoric statues by Stanislav Sucharda. A stylized crown tops the tower and lent the building its name. The insurance company also changed its name to Koruna. A double passageway runs through the ground floor. A cupola tops the point where the two passageway arms meet, a fine example of Secession architecture formed from thousands of glass shaped pieces.

A large buffet with fast food was opened here in 1931 in place of a café. It offered fast hot and cold refreshments and was wildly popular amongst Prague's citizens and visitors alike. It functioned here until the start of the 1990s when the building underwent intensive reconstruction. When repairs ended in 1996 it was a big surprise that Koruna's buffet was gone for good. Now it holds boutiques, brand name fashion stores, a café, pizzeria and the largest audio electronics shop in Prague.

36 House of the Black Madonna
◈ 50°5'13.30"N, 14°25'31.84"E

At the start of the 20th century, new directions in visual art started being chartered, including Cubism. It caught the eye of not just painters but soon architects, amongst them Josef Gočár. He created a project for which space was created by razing the Baroque House of the Black Madonna (or the House at the Golden Grate). Thus Prague's first Cubist house was built on Celetná street in 1912. It kept its predecessor's name and a statue of the Black Madonna with Jesus behind a golden grate. The new department store with its modern appearance fits in very well with local buildings. It's most famous for its second-floor Grand Café Orient. This exceptional café, visited by a number of artists, met its fate after WWI, and gradually the entire building's function transformed. The entire building was fully reconstructed in 1993–94 for the Museum of Czech Cubism. Further repairs came in the fresh new 21st century. The Grand Café Orient was reopened in 2005, and is utterly unique in the world. It was furnished based on several preserved black and white photos from its heyday with replicas of the original furniture and chandeliers.

37 Villa Müller
◆ 50°5'33.33"N, 14°22'42.45"E

In the 1920s and 1930s, Czechoslovakia saw a remarkable boom in family home construction. Prague was no exception, and one may find for example a number of luxury villas in green city quarters. The most important one in Prague and the country is the functionalist Müller villa in Střešovice, built in 1928-30 based on design of famous architect Adolf Loos (1870–1933) with help of architect Karl Lhota for the family of engineer František Müller, co-owner of the construction company Kapsa and Müller. Adolf Loos also designed the household facilities, all of its furnishings, lights, etc. He even designed the garden landscaping in cooperation with three landscape architects. The villa, seeming rather austere from the outside, employs Loos' theory of a so-called Raumplan (spatial plan), i.e. dividing individual areas into various height levels, phased together and interconnected by stairs, and abandoning classic house floor separation. The author himself declared that it was his most splendid work. Today it's one of his most completely preserved works. The villa was declared a national cultural monument in 1995 and placed under care of the City of Prague Museum. One part of the house holds the Adolf Loos Study and Documentation Centre, which among other activities engages in research and interpretation of the architect's work and that of his students and protégés; it organizes lectures, meetings of experts in architecture or visual arts, etc.

38 The Dancing House
⌖ 50°4'31.60"N, 14°24'50.75"E

A victim of the bombing of Prague occurring on Valentines Day in 1945 led to the birth of a corner building along Rašínovo nábřeží by the Vltava. With the bombsite finally cleared, the plot remained completely empty from 1960 on. Many proposals came for its use, but the final decision came in 1992, when the grounds were finally sold to the Dutch insurance company Nationale Nederlanden. Based on the design of world-famous architects Vlado Milunić and Frank Owen Gehry, a true original was born from 1994 to 1996, having two underground and 8 above-ground floors. Its building evoked a huge discussion on modern architecture with emphatic voices for and against. For years it has been known as the Dancing House or Ginger and Fred, the names of the American dance partners between World Wars. Ginger Rogers was the inspiration for the glass tower, and Fred Astair for the stone tower. "His" tower is topped with a jellyfish-like copula. Mostly offices, but also a luxurious café and restaurant, are found inside. The underground and ground-floor space can be leased, including a conference hall for fifty persons with moving wall. Some of the interior areas were designed by Eva Jiřičná, a famous architect and designer of Czech decent straddling the border between the Czech Republic and Great Britain. The Czech magazine Architect named it one of the five most interesting building events of the 1990s in the Czech Republic. It also won America's Time Magazine Design of the Year 1996.

Technical Monuments

39 Astronomical Clock
◈ 50°5'13.22"N, 14°25'14.57"E

Very few visitors to Prague haven't stood at least once before Old Town Hall and waited for the clock to reach the top of the hour to see the moving figures of the famous Astronomical Clock or "Orloj". It is a unique technical and artistic monument that underwent extraordinary development over its six centuries of often threatened existence. It was built by Mikuláš of Kadaň in 1410. Clockmaker Ludvík Hainz saved the Orloj in the 19th century, when he got it back up and running after many years of disrepair. It was also threatened in May 1945 during a fire in Old Town Hall; some figures were completed destroyed. The monument has three parts. In the upper part in two windows the 12 Apostles appear one by one with their attributes on the hour. Sculptor and puppeteer Vojtěch Sucharda created today's figures in 1948. Other (allegoric) figures also become animated on the sides of the clock – Death, the Turk, the Miser and Vanity. After the windows close the rooster crows, and thus ends this so eagerly awaited, yet short presentation. Other inanimate figures appear on either side of the calendar – Philosopher, Astronomer, Chronicler and Michael the Archangel. The central astronomical part of Orloj measures and displays several different types of time based on an astrolabe. The calendar, the Orloj's youngest part, is the work of Josef Mánes from 1865. The center of the calendar displays Old Town's coat-of-arms; twelve large medallions allegorically create individual months of the year, with twelve small signs of the zodiac.

40 Loreto – Chimes
50°5'21.34"N, 14°23'30.71"E

A wondrous technical monument stirring the interest of passersby since the end of the 17th century is located inside the Loreto clock tower embrasure. These chimes comprised of thirty larger and smaller bells play a three-minute melody of the Marian song *We Greet You a Thousand Times* from 8:00 a.m. to 6:00 p.m. on the hour. The bells were cast in Amsterdam, and clockmaker Petr Neumann arranged them into chimes here in Prague. Lesser Side businessman Eberhard of Glauchov paid for everything and dedicated it to Loreto out of being grateful that his daughter, ill with the plague, recovered. A major celebration accompanied consecration of the bells in 1695, with members of an important noble family becoming their godfathers. The first bell gained the highest benefactor – Emperor Leopold I – on August 15 that year on the day marking the Assumption of Mary, and the chimes – a modern technological wonder – played for the first time. It has two systems – the melody originates by hammers striking up to 27 static bells, in part using the clock mechanism, and in part the musician may control keys ranging up to two and a half octaves and play any melody. Important personalities playing them in the past include Wolfgang Amadeus Mozart and Franz Liszt, and concerts are still held. The chimes underwent repair in the 1990s to ensure that all people walking or standing nearby can enjoy the music.

41 Petřín Observation Tower and Funicular

⌖ 50°4′57.72″N, 14°23′58.21″E

TECHNICAL MONUMENTS

The World Jubilee Exhibition took place in Prague in 1891. Thanks to the initiative of the Czech Tourist Club and their enthusiasm for the Eiffel Tower, an observation tower was built that is its similar yet five-times smaller twin. The tower was put up in no time; the project was prepared in 1890 and funding was gathered, building started in March 1891, and by that August 20 the observation tower welcomed its first guests. The octagonal steel frame is 60 meters tall. Two staircases lead to the platform at 51 meters, each with 299 stairs, one for going up and the other for coming down. A crown originally decorated the roof, later replaced by a TV antenna. It served for broadcasting TV signals until 1992. It didn't see major reconstruction until 1999–2002. Since then it has a new ground floor with entrance hall, buffet and Czech Tourist Club exhibit. Upon resolving the vision of building Petřín's new observation tower, engineers were already speculating on how to bring visitors up to it. The solution was by funicular, or incline. This too was built swiftly, with its first ride up taking place on July 25, 1891. The route measured 400 m, and the equipment used water balanced propulsion. Operations were interrupted during WWI and for long thereafter. It wasn't until 1931 that a new funicular was built, this time with electric propulsion. The track was lengthened to 511 m. Operation ceased once again for many years (1965–1985) due to track damage from water and slumping of the hillside. But today it reliably takes travelers up to Petřín and back down again.

42 Žižkov Tower
50°4'51.77"N, 14°27'4.06"E

Prague was once given the attribute "City of a Hundred Spires". But there are actually several hundred larger and smaller ones. But one is the tallest and is visible from practically every spot in the city – the television broadcast tower at Žižkov, from which over ten television and a similar amount of radio stations broadcast. Like many modern structures, this one has evoked stormy discussions and even loud protests by the public. People question its esthetic value, functionality and ecological safety, and its erection at a part of an old Jewish cemetery was also fought. Despite this, it was completed and brought into operation in 1992. The 1980s project was compiled by a collective of authors led by Václav Aulický and engineers Alex Bém and Jiří Kozák. The entire design is formed of three tubes. The tallest of them with the largest diameter (6.4 meters) and reaching 216 meters high with antenna contains two high-speed elevators. The other two are more narrow (4.8 meters in diameter) and measure 134 meters. All three bear three cabins – at a height of 66 meters you can visit a restaurant, which is also a great place for holding various social events, trainings, etc. At 93 meters you can get a great view of Prague and far beyond. You can see things up to 100 kilometers away in good weather. The restaurant and lookout tower are open every day. In 2000, the austere structure was enlivened with the appearance of 10 giant crawling babies, created by artist David Černý. After a few months the babies disappeared, but because they were so popular, they returned about a year later and crawl up it to this day.

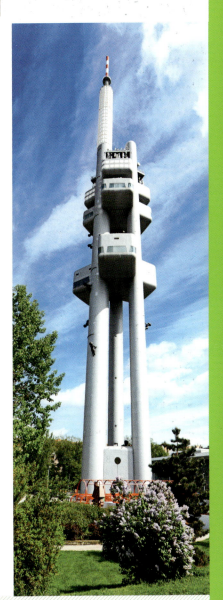

43 Podolí Water Treatment Plant
✣ 50°3'25.88"N, 14°25'11.87"E

People have always had the problem of gaining access to water and distributing it. As societies develop there's an ever-growing need for more. There were several water plants in Prague in the 19th century, but their capacity didn't cover need. Architect Antonín Engel designed a project according to which a large capacity filtration water plant was built in 1925-29. It was comprised of several buildings – the largest of which was the filtration hall, along with the administrative building and other operations buildings. A second filtration hall in the same Neo-Classicist style was added in the latter-1950s based on designs by Antonín Engel and Maxmilián Koschin. A 45-meter water tower rises in the middle. The façade above the portal is decorated with statues by several authors, which allegorically illustrate the River Vltava and its tributaries, the Vydra, Otava, the Šumava's Blanice, Malše, Berounka, Sázava, Vlašim's Blanice, Želivka, Lužnice and the Nežárka. The equipment and technologies at the water treatment plant at Podolí have been constantly modernized over the years providing ever-increasing output. Water from the Vltava is mixed here with water from the Želivka and Jizera Rivers, and supplies Old Town and Josefov. It also serves as a reserve water supply. It has a standard output of 500 liters per second that can be increased to 2,200 liters. 1992 saw general overhauls during operation of buildings, and modernization of technological equipment. A building was also added into which the Prague Waterworks Museum moved. The entire historically, architecturally and technically valuable complex is a protected monument.

44 Prague Main Train Station
 50°4'58.95"N, 14°26'9.03"E

TECHNICAL MONUMENTS

There is an entire series of train stations and station buildings in Prague. The oldest is the Main Train Station. Its latter-19th century construction was driven by the need to connect the existing track with the Prague–Vienna line and Prague's station at the time. A Neo-Renaissance railway building appeared in 1871 where the Main Train Station now stands, named after Emperor Franz Joseph I. Both passenger and freight trains continued increasing in number. By the century's end it was clear that the existing station wasn't capable of handling such large volume, so a new station had to be built. A tender was announced in which renowned architects placed their bid. Josef Fanta won the tender. His design was implemented in 1901–09, and the rails, underground passages and halls were repaired during full operation. Fanta's building is Prague's largest Secession structure. The central hall has a large semi-circular window above the entrance. The entrance is covered by a metal, Secession-shaped construction and two towers with glass domes rising on the sides. Statues by important Czech sculptors adorn the façade, tower and hall, and the south tower holds a clock. The interiors also hold paintings and sculptures. Two sidelong, symmetrical wings now boast restaurants, offices, accommodations, a representation hall and erstwhile imperial, later presidential parlor with wood paneling, Secession furnishing and wall decorations. Two steel-frame arches cover the train platforms. Prague main train station is a Prague and Czech Republic main railway centre where stop all regional and fast trains. From Prague main train station you can go everywhere in Czech Republic and Europe as well.

45 Sewage Treatment Plant in Bubeneč
50°6'36.43"N, 14°24'7.87"E

Humankind has been resolving the problem of draining wastewater since time immemorial. It was no different in Prague either. In the 1880s, Prague's city council decided that it must take a complex and systematic approach to resolving this. It held two consecutive tenders, but no winner came out of them. The solution eventually implemented came from a foreign expert with vast experience in building similar waterworks and sewerage facilities, Sir William Heerlein Lindley. He located the new sewerage treatment plant in Bubeneč, making perfect use of the rising terrain. Even the distance of the locality was regarded as beneficial. Building began in 1901, test operation of a three-stage sewerage treatment plant began in 1906. Prague's sewers, totaling around 90 km at the time, emptied into the plant. By the 1920s, full capacity was reached and it was expanded. It then served reliably until 1967, when a new mechanical-biological treatment plant opened on the island Císařský ostrov. In the 1980s, a group of people appeared who realized what a unique example of industrial architecture lay in Bubeneč, and they were successful in getting the entire complex inscribed as a national cultural monument. They then began to implement their idea to create within these historical environs the Eco-technical Museum. Visitors here can see the inlet crypt, they pass through a sand trap, through the largest underground structure, through other areas on to ten sediment tanks, and then explore the machine room. It is most popular during such events as *Water Day* in March, *Unlocking the Canals* in April, etc. The monument however is also used for commercial purposes, it holds exhibitions, lectures and conferences, and movies are filed here.

Museums and Galleries

46 National Museum
⊕ 50°4'44.31"N, 14°25'51.32"E

The national museum as an institution is the largest state museum in the Czech Republic with collection, scientific, cultural and methodical functions. It engages in many varied fields of natural and social science. It grew out of the Patriotic Museum in Bohemia founded in 1818 thanks to provincial aristocrats, and mainly paleontologist and mineralogist Count Kašpar of Šternberk. Czech aristocrats donated their private collections to form the museum's core. NM's main seat is an historic building, a national cultural monument standing at the head of Wenceslas Square. Architect Josef Schulz won the tender for its design in 1883. The Neo-Renaissance structure was built in 1885–90. The day's greatest artists took part on its adornment, thematically centered on Czech history. The National Museum has many other buildings: the former seat of Radio Free Europe (previously the Federal Assembly), the National Monument in Vítkov, the Náprstek Museum, the Czech Museum of Music and museums outside Prague. The museum also holds a library. The main museum holds the library's general part and the department of manuscripts and old prints. A unique collection of historic and current newspapers and magazines is kept at the Governor's Summer Palace in Prague's Stromovka.

47 City of Prague Museum
50°5'23.86"N, 14°26'18.53"E

Museums began to proliferate as natural and social sciences developed, especially history, but also in relation to latter-19th century patriotism (here and abroad). So it's no wonder that the idea came to create a city museum to document Prague's historical and cultural development. Historian, teacher and politician Wácslaw Wladiwoj Tomek greatly contributed to its creation. The oldest collections were located in the café pavilion at Na Poříčí. But they grew until the building no longer sufficed; a new museum had to be built. Antonín Balšánek led the Neo-Renaissance project in 1896–98. Here you may see the relief History with Art, Science and Crafts Form the Glory of our Past by Ladislav Šaloun, at the top of which is also his statue Prague Allegory. The building's center holds a vestibule with staircase, and the exhibiting halls are found in the wings. The museum's most important and valuable exhibit is a model of Prague from 1826–37 made out of paperboard by Antonín Langweil. In a unique manner, he captured the exact likeness of over 2,000 structures in historic parts of Prague including minute details such as windows, house signs, various decorative elements, façade colors, etc. The fact that around half the buildings have since been lost or rebuilt makes this model all the more precious. You can see it in digitalized form in the 3D cinema.

48 Vítkov National Monument
50°5'18.65"N, 14°26'59.91"E

The fact that Prague lies in a basin and on hills surrounding it makes room for many dominant features. The National Monument on Vítkov Hill, later renamed Žižkov, is one of them. It is said to have the largest bronze equestrian statue in the world, which represents the Hussite commander Jan Žižka of Trocnov. Here under his leadership, the Hussite army won a battle with the crusaders on July 14, 1420. Bohumil Kafka authored the huge statue. He started in 1931 and spent 11 years, and parts of had to be hidden during the occupation. It wasn't emplaced until 1950, eight years after its author's passing. But a national monument by architect Jan Zázvorka stood here much earlier here in 1928–32, in honor of the legionnaires and the foundation of the Czechoslovak Republic. The massive block construction with granite sheeting became a Wehrmacht storage site during WWII. Urns of fallen soldiers from both World Wars are kept in a special hall. The area is decorated with mosaics by Max Švabinský and the statue Wounded by Jan Štursa. The entire complex was reconstructed starting in 2007, and began serving a cultural center in October 2009. It holds concerts, theater presentations, concerts and exhibitions. An exhibit opened in October 2009 called the *Crossroads of Czech and Czechoslovak Statehood*. The café here makes for a pleasant visit, in which various cultural and social events are also held.

49 Museum of Decorative Arts
◈ 50°5'23.57"N, 14°24'59.09"E

The Museum of Decorative Arts in Prague is among those museums founded in the second half of the 19th century, generally thanks to collectors and patrons with patriotic sentiment. Its task today is researching history of Czech and foreign applied arts, design, fashion creation, literary culture or photography and its presentation. The Prague Chamber of Trade and Commerce, its president Bohumil Bondy, and mainly the knight Vojtěch Lanna made huge donations to the museum. Lanna is to thank for one of the largest collections of rare glass. A very important gift given to the museum by the Waldes family in 1995 is the so-called Karlštejn treasure – 387 pieces of art from the time of Charles IV. The museum's history dates back to 1885, first exhibiting in the Rudolfinum. A new museum was built across from it in French Renaissance style in 1897–98 by design of Josef Schulz. The interior and exterior adornments are highly ostentatious. Today it holds the permanent exhibit Stories of Materials and occasional exhibitions are also held here. The museum tries to present new trends in its exhibiting – like post-modern applied art in 1990 or creation by Czech artists who've established themselves abroad, foreign greats in their fields, as well as exhibitions from their own collections (Secession, Cubism, Art Deco, posters, photography). It also systematically presents exhibits from the area of design.

50 National Gallery – Trade Fair Palace
50°6'4.39"N, 14°25'56.78"E

An interesting functionalist building belonging to the National Gallery has stood in Prague since 1928. It was built by designs of architects Oldřich Tyl and Josef Fuchs. The purpose of its construction was to develop a commercial center in the new republic and exhibit products of local companies. Here in the autumn of 1928 it even saw the display of Mucha's The Slav Epic, for which an adequate place has yet to be found in Prague. Jews hid here during WWII to keep from being sent to concentration camps. The palace served its original mission until 1949, after which it became the seat of several foreign trade companies. It burnt down in 1974 and the damage was so great that it was slated for demolition. This luckily didn't occur; architect Miroslav Masák's design was used to rebuild it and make it home to the National Gallery. It didn't open until 1995. The 20th and 21st-century permanent exhibit shows the development of Czech and foreign visual art in continuity of the past two centuries. The exhibit presents work of key authors of Czech visual arts in monographic profiles or in selection of well-suited works and works by foreign authors. The image of the times is enhanced by examples of architecture, furniture, artistic crafts, fashion, design and scenography. It also has photography, drawings and graphics, concentrated in the graphics displays. Aside from famous personalities, it also features other forgotten and unknown artists.

51 Kampa Museum
◈ 50°5'1.81"N, 14°24'30.90"E

The history of Sova's Mills on Kampa dates back to the 14th century. The mill, altered many times, functioned here until the end of the 19th century when it burnt down. Part was completely razed due to regulation of the Vltava, but a dilapidated residence remained standing at the start of the new millennium. The building was generously reconstructed starting in 2000. Meda and Jan Mládek donated their collection of modern art created in the Czech Republic. A major flood in 2002 prevented the museum's ceremonial opening and heavily damaged the newly repaired complex. The gallery opened in 2003. Its visitors now have the unique opportunity to see the greatest and most comprehensive collection of the works of František Kupka, a group of 17 sculptures by Otto Gutfreund, over 240 works by Jiří Kolář, as well as visual works by many other Czech, Slovak, Polish, Hungarian and Yugoslavian artists. Jiří and Běla Kolář also dedicated their collection to Kampa Museum, including the Collection for Jindřich Chalupecký. The museum makes these collections accessible to the public and also holds many short-term exhibitions of Czech and foreign artists, including recent presentations of works by Yoko Ono, Frank Malina, Joseph Beuys, Matěj Krén, Julian Opie, Piet Mondrian, Theodor Pištěk and Andy Warhol.

52 Museum of Public Transportation in Prague
◈ 50°5'39.39"N, 14°23'17.77"E

In Střešovice, there is one of Prague's early depots built in 1909. In the early 1990s, it became a cultural monument and ceased operations. It was the perfect choice however for a different purpose – it became a museum in 1993, accumulating a collection of tramcars going back as far as 1929. It also displays buses, trolleybuses, one metro car and other exhibits – conductor uniforms, tickets, photos, columns at stops, etc. The most valuable exhibit is the summer car for the horse-drawn track from 1886, also rare are the first electrified cars from the turn of the 20th century or the mayor's parlor car from 1900. The depot's original function has also been partially retained – from spring to autumn on weekends and holidays, old cars from nostalgic line no. 91 ride out to the city center.

Cultural Institutions

53 National Theater
◆ 50°4'51.09"N, 14°24'50.76"E

The desire of Czechs to have their own theater with presentations in Czech grew ever stronger in the 19th century. After several half-hearted attempts, the Czech patriotic circles finally found success – grounds were bought, a money collection was announced, where members of all levels of society contributed, including the ruler itself, and finally it came to tender. Architect Josef Zítek won and designed it in Northern Italian Renaissance style. The cornerstone was laid in 1868 and in 1881 the theater was ceremoniously opened with Smetana's opera, *Libuše*. A fire occurred that same year, but by taking up yet another collection, it was opened in all its beauty in 1883. Architect Josef Schulz was entrusted with its repairs. A wide range of artists decorated it, dubbed the "National Theater Generation". They included Bohuslav Schnirch, Josef Václav Myslbek, Vojtěch Hynais, Mikoláš Aleš, František Ženíšek and many others. From the creative aspect, the most admirable part is the main foyer and the President's Box with adjacent parlors. All three repertoires perform in the historic building – opera, theatre and ballet. The theater is 26 meters high and has very good acoustics – even in the upper levels. Above the stage hangs a two-ton chandelier that is 3 meters wide and 5.5 meters long with 260 lights. It is serviced in the attic area, where it can be moved based on need. Three curtains hang between the stage and the seats. The theater also features a pipe organ.

54 Theater of the Estates
50°5'9.52"N, 14°25'25.25"E

CULTURAL INSTITUTIONS

Count František Antonín Nostic-Rieneck had this theater built 100 years before the National Theater. His heirs sold the theater to the Czech Estates, hence the name. Architect Antonín Haffenecker created the blueprints for this Classicist-style building. It was constructed in 1781–83. The theater is closely related to Wolfgang Amadeus Mozart, whose operas *Don Giovanni* and *La clemenza di Tito* had their world premiere here in Prague (1787 and 1791) under the author's baton. For the first time in the play *Fidlovačka* the song *Where Is My Home* was heard, scored by Františka Škroupa to lyrics by Josef Kajetán Tyl. It later became the Czechoslovak (now Czech) national anthem. Now this theater, remarkably preserved in its original likeness, is one of the venues of the National Theater, and features mainly drama. This is the traditional main venue for Mozart's works, and is the only existing Prague theater where he worked. The rotating stage reaches a width and depth of 18 m. Two of the most important boxes are the Emperor's Box and President's Box.

55 State Opera

◇ 50°4'49.58"N, 14°25'58.70"E

The Czech National Theater was built in 1868. Prague's German population also longed for a theater they could call their own, so after meetings commenced in 1883 a plan came to build a new theater building. The Viennese company Fellner and Helmer drew up the plans. The representative New German Theater's opening ceremony in 1888 showcased the opera The Master Singers of Nuuremberg by Richard Wagner. Opera presentations fare outweighed other repertoires. Many fantastic conductors and interpreters playing here, including the famous Enrico Caruso and other stars of the day. In the 1920s and 1930s during the time of the gathering Nazi danger, the New German Theater in Prague was a democratic sanctuary where artists gathered, whose work in neighboring Germany was undesirable for their advanced opinions or ethnic origin. In 1945, the German "Deutsches Theater" was renamed to the Czech Theater of the Fifth of May, then the Smetana Theater, becoming the National Theater's third venue.

56 Rudolfinum
50°5′23.85″N, 14°24′55.66″E

Behind the National Theater and National Museum, the House of Artists or Rudolfinum (named after the successor to the Austrian throne, Archduke Rudolf) is the third most important architectural undertaking in the second half of the 19th century. The Czech Savings Bank had the Rudolfinum built to mark the 50th anniversary since its founding. It asked Archduke Rudolf if it could name the structure after him, the heir to the Habsburg throne. A spot was selected on the eastern bank of the Vltava called Rejdiště. A lovely Neo-Renaissance building was built in 1876–84 by design of architects Josef Zítek and Josef Schulz, to be used for concerts and holding exhibits. It lost this function temporarily in the years 1918–1939 and 1945–1946, when the Parliament of the Czechoslovak Republic assembled here. But the first year of the Prague Spring festival was held here in 1946, and the Rudolfinum again became and has remained the seat of the Czech Philharmonic. The spacious Dvořák Room has fantastic acoustics, and you'll also find here a very high-quality pipe organ from the end of the 19th century. The Suk Room beside it serves as a chamber concert venue. During extensive reconstruction in the 1990s, exhibition areas were restored in the northern part, where the Rudolfinum Gallery now resides, a part of the Museum of Decorative Arts. Since 1994, it has specialized in contemporary visual art, already earning a very solid reputation both home and abroad.

57 Klementinum
50°5'12.05"N, 14°24'57.15"E

Jesuits came to Prague in 1556 at the invitation of Emperor Ferdinand I and began building their college here at the spot of a Dominican monastery. The complex of school and sacral buildings was built until the mid-18th century thanks to such important Baroque architects as Kilián Ignác Dientzenhofer and František Maxmilián Kaňka. No less famous artists decorated the interior, such as Petr Brandl, Matyáš Bernard Braun, Václav Vavřinec Reiner and others. It housed part of Charles University and its library from the 17th to the 19th century. Architect Ladislav Machoň authored its modern modification (1920s). He raised the building at Křížovnická street and restored the complex for the needs of the university library. Aside from today's National Library with its 6 million volumes including old manuscripts and prints, the Klementinum also has three churches (Church of the Holy Saviour, the Wallachian Chapel and Church of St. Clement), a number of lovely historic halls and the Astronomical Tower. The Church of the Holy Saviour is considered one of the most precious early Baroque monuments in Prague, and was once the main Jesuit church in Bohemia. The local astronomical observatory became the basis in 1953 of the Astronomical Institute of the Czech Academy of Sciences. Meteorological measuring started here in 1775 and continues today. It holds occasional exhibits, concerts, lectures, forums and other cultural events.

58 Municipal House
⌖ 50°5'15.60"N, 14°25'39.94"E

CULTURAL INSTITUTIONS

Prague is rich in its Secession monuments. The most important structure in this style is the Municipal House. Built in 1905–11, this representative building gave ground to the Czech commons at a symbolic place of Czech statehood. That is, a royal seat stood here stood here, the so-called King's Court. Czechoslovakia's independence was declared from here in 1918. Architects Antonín Balšánek and Osvald Polívka designed a new, multi-functional building. All meaningful personalities in the world of visual arts (Ladislav Šaloun, František Ženíšek, Jan Preisler, Alfons Mucha and others) shared in its ostentatious, invaluable embellishment. The sophistication of its technical infrastructure was unprecedented. The building held 1,200 rooms, the largest of which is the concert Smetana Hall for an audience of up to 1,200 people. It is the venue for example of *Prague Spring* concerts and pipe organ concerts. There are restaurants, a café, pub, wine bar, a number of exquisite halls, used for exhibitions, balls or other social events (Grégr, Palacký and Mayor's Halls), or smaller parlors such as the Moravian Slovak, Conductors and Oriental Parlors. The building is also highly noteworthy for its series of technical wonders: electric elevators, remote-controlled air handling system, central vacuuming, pneumatic post and a modern telephone switchboard.

59 Hybernia Theater

50°5'14.55"N, 14°25'43.53"E

Across from the Powder Gate and Municipal House stands the Hybernia Theater, which opened in 2006 after complete renovation of the building. The Empire appearance of the house U Hybernů came during reconstruction in 1808–11. Until that time, a Baroque church had stood here belonging to a monastery of Irish Franciscans – the "Hyberns", terminated by Emperor Joseph II in 1785 like so many others. At the turn of the 19th century when the building belonged to Count Jan Sweerts-Sporck, it was a place of theater, which seemed to foretell its current use. After the mentioned Empire redesign, it housed the financial authority, customs office and other offices. Following early WWII modification that continued after a post-war pause, the House U Hybernů hosted many various exhibitions. Today it serves cultural purposes, mainly for musicals, but also for classical and popular music concerts as well as drama presentations of ensembles near and far. It also holds exhibitions or various company events, congresses and presentations.

Natural Monuments

60 Zoo
⊕ 50°7′0.15″N, 14°24′39.58″E

A modern zoological garden in Prague's Troja spreads over more than 60 hectares, visited by over a million visitors each year. It has a relatively long history. Efforts to create a zoo in Prague appeared in the 1880s, though without success. Preparations for a realistic project began after the creation of the Czechoslovak state. Landowner Alois Svoboda donated eight hectares of land in Troja for this purpose, and zoologist and ornithologist Jiří Janda managed its establishment. He also became the zoo's first director. The zoo's opening ceremony took place on September 28, 1931, when it had around 200 animals. From its outset, it has successfully maintained a herd of Przewalski horses, and in 1960, it was entrusted with maintaining the breed's international studbook. Over time, Prague Zoo has grown both in the quantity of animals (now nearly 700 species and 5,500 animals), and in size. However, in 2002, just like the all of Prague and a major part of the CR, it was hit by a devastating flood, affecting half of its entire area. A seal named Gaston came to symbolize this catastrophe, having swum all the way to Germany only to die before being rescued. Many other animals also drown or had to be euthenized, and many others were evacuated. The decimated zoo soon began to thrive however, and since then, it has seen the growth of a series of new, very modern pavilions, many others were reconstructed in grand fashion, and building is still continuing. The most popular include the Africa House, the Gorilla Pavilion, the Sichuan House, the Indonesian Jungle, and the new Elephant House and further exhibits are under construction The zoo also hosts many supporting programs, such as commented feeding and training with certain types of animals (e.g. penguins, camels, seals, moose, Przewalski horses), evening guided zoo tours, etc. The "Obora" Observation Tower opened in 2009. It stands 18.5 meters high and lends a lovely view of the zoo and the entire city.

61 Prague Botanical Garden
50°7'9.62"N, 14°24'46.51"E

NATURAL MONUMENTS

You can combine visiting the zoo with a tour of the nearby Prague Botanical Garden, which lies in very rugged terrain. Though established in 1969, for years it remained inaccessible and only served scientific experiments. It eventually opened to the public in 1992, and it is by all means worthy of visiting. In its center are annual and perennial flowerbeds, where by spring, something is always blooming. Here stands a rock garden greenhouse with plants from Southeast Asia, the Mediterranean, New Zealand and Australia. Visitors will be thrilled by the Japanese garden with a diminutive stream and lake, Japanese maples, rhododendrons and bamboo. Lying adjacent to outdoor complex is St. Claire's Vineyard with chapel and old vineyard home. In the garden's outer lying area in the rocky terrain of the southern slope on the Troja side, the tropical green house Fata Morgana opened in 2004, divided into three sections – dry tropics and subtropics, lowland rain forest and a harsh high mountain environment. It is unique for not only what it contains but also for its S-shaped ground plan and original design.

62 Wallenstein Garden
⊕ 50°5'23.58"N, 14°24'25.98"E

A large garden lies adjacent the Wallenstein Palace and Wallenstein Riding Hall, 1.7 hectares in size and surrounded on the other sides by a high wall. The origin of the palace and garden dates back to the 1620s. Nicolo Sebregondi elaborated the design of the early-Baroque, purely geometrically articulated garden. The sala terrene, decorated by frescoes and stuccowork, serves as a summer venue for various cultural events – concerts and theatrical performances. Beside it rises the grotto, an artificial stalactite cave, and on the right, there is an exotic bird aviary. The flower gardens with bronze fountain and a statue of *Venus with Cupid* (copy) fills the space before the buildings. In the other parts of the garden, you can sit by a pond containing various species of fish, on the island stands a marble statue of Hercules and the Naiads, a copy of the work by Adriaena de Vries. In 1648, Swedish forces took away as war treasure another group of statues based on Greek Mythology by the same author. Here you can admire their copies. Like many other of Prague's historical monuments, the garden was generally reconstructed at the start of the new millennium.

63 Stromovka
50°5'15.60"N, 14°25'39.94"E

The royal preserve here, today better known as Stromovka, has quite a long history. Allegedly founded by Přemysl Otakar II in 1266, it has undergone several periods of flourishing and demise over in the centuries. It got so bad in the 18th century that it was nearly eliminated altogether. Ultimately, thanks to Count Kinský, it was restored once again, and opened to the public in 1804. Since that time, it has slowly emerged as a landscaped English park with lovely flower gardens, ponds and statue adornment, its days as hunting grounds long gone. Even recently however, Stromovka's existence was threatened. It was heavily damaged in 2002 by flooding, which took out several hundred trees and led to its closing until April 2003. The park then gradually began to reemerge, new trees have been planted, and there are grown trees of species that stood fast during the flood (e.g. lindens, ash, oaks) Exotic trees are only found above the flood line. It is, however, being negatively impacted by construction of the Blanka Tunnel, a future part of Prague's Ring Road. Today, Stromovka covers 95 hectares in size, and serves mainly for recreation. The so-called Oak Hillock is the remains of an island from the former Great Pond, once fed by the Vltava via the so-called Rudolf's tunnel. Another monument is the former Royal Hall from the end of the 17th century, restored into a garden restaurant a century later. Restaurateur Václav Šlechta began renting it in the 1880s, under whose name it became famous as a popular trip destination of Praguers. Today it impatiently awaits reconstruction.

64 Gardens under Prague Castle
50°5'30.34"N, 14°24'24.77"E

On the hillside beneath Prague Castle spread the so-called palace gardens, connecting the Castle with the Lesser Side. They formed after the loss in the 16th century of the function of the fortified castle system; the same applied to the castle's South Gardens. These grounds gradually came to be owned by aristocrats and rich townsmen; larger units were formed, market gardens and later vineyards morphed into Italian-style ornamental gardens. However, the Swedes conquered and plundered the Lesser Side in 1648. After a period of ruin, the gardens began to come back to life. Their owners restored them, this time in Baroque style. The balustrade terraces are accessible along steep staircases ending with balconies, decorated by statues and fountains. They hold clinging plants, roses and other types of flowers, grape vines, as well as many trees and shrubs. Most gardens contain gallery halls and various pavilions. Five palace gardens are interconnected: the Ledebour, Small and Great Pálffy, Kolovrat and Small Fürstenberk Gardens, they are accessible from Valdštejnská street, from the Old Castle Stairs or from the garden Na Valech. The Great Fürstenberk Garden has a separate entrance from the Old Castle Stairs, and was last open to the public in 2008.

Especially in the spring, when everything is in bloom, the gardens are simply spectacular. Evening strolls through the illuminated gardens are equally as enchanting. The gardens saw complete reconstruction starting in the 1990s and lasting two decades, and gradually opened to the public. Building and landscape garden architects seeing to their restoration worked on shaping the gardens based on Langweil's model of Prague from 1826–36.